Arcaen

OrangeBooks Publication

1st Floor, Rajhans Arcade, Mall Road, Kohka, Bhilai, Chhattisgarh 490020

Website: **www.orangebooks.in**

© Copyright, 2025, Author

All rights reserved. No part of this book may be reproduced, stored in a retrieval system, or transmitted, in any form by any means, electronic, mechanical, magnetic, optical, chemical, manual, photocopying, recording or otherwise, without the prior written consent of its writer.

First Edition, 2025

ISBN: 978-93-6554-092-5

Arcaen

EDITORS
SNIGDHA BHATT
ASMITA SHARMA

OrangeBooks Publication
www.orangebooks.in

Editor's Note

Folklore is a living, breathing tapestry of stories passed down through generations, shaped by time, place and the diverse voices of the people who tell them. As editors, we are acutely aware of the multiplicity and fluidity inherent in folkloric narratives. A single story can manifest in countless versions, each reflecting different cultural nuances, regional variations, and individual interpretations. No one tale holds a singular truth; instead, folklore is a mosaic, evolving with each retelling.

This book is not intended to offend the sentiments of any individual or group, but rather to celebrate the richness of folklore in its many forms. The goal is to offer a compilation of some versions of well-known tales, while respecting the diversity of voices that shape them. We acknowledge that there may be differences in the versions presented here—some tales may echo similar themes yet diverge in key details or interpretations. This is the very essence of folklore: stories told and retold, adapting to new generations and circumstances.

In showcasing these variations, we hope to honour the broad spectrum of folklore traditions, while encouraging readers to engage with these stories in a spirit of curiosity and respect. We believe that by embracing the multiplicity of narratives, we gain a deeper understanding of the cultures that bring these tales to life, and the profound ways in which stories shape our collective imagination.

With this in mind, we invite you to explore the tales within these pages with an open heart, aware of the myriad voices that have contributed to their telling.

Preface

India's folkloric tradition resembles an intricate tapestry of beliefs, narratives and established customs, which are deeply interwoven into the nation's diverse cultural milieu. These traditions extend beyond storytelling and function as essential vehicles for the transmission of shared values, ethical principles and cultural identity. As it manifests in oral traditions, myths, fables and rituals, folklore has significantly contributed to the intricate social fabric of Indian society. Oral narratives, for instance, serve a dual purpose as both entertainment and conduits for traditional knowledge, facilitating the intergenerational transfer of cultural heritage. Folkloric accounts often intersect with spiritual beliefs, exemplifying the convergence of divine and mundane realms, while rituals provide insights into the social and communal structures that govern daily life.

Folklore has a profound formative influence on cultural comprehension. During one's developmental years, exposure to narratives conveyed by elder family members—tales of the exploits and adventures of similar characters, their ethical dilemmas and the complex interplay between humans and their environment—deeply ingrains societal values and cultural beliefs. These narratives instil virtues of bravery and compassion while establishing the importance of kinship within cultural groups. Furthering, via their intensely captivating nature a sense of cultural identity and ancestral connection. Recurrent motifs of affection, self-sacrifice and perseverance significantly shape individual outlooks and aspirations, contributing to the construction of a personal identity, philosophy and goal.

The diverse nature of Indian folklore highlights the multifaceted character of its society. Every region possesses a unique set of legends and characters, shaped by local customs, linguistic nuances, and historical backgrounds. From the local vernacular oral tales to numerous versions of the Mahabharata and Ramayana along with the moral-laden tales of the Panchatantra, these narratives reflect complex social interactions within the Indian cultures. This variety not only showcases the subcontinent's rich cultural heritage but also demonstrates how these stories can be adapted to fit contemporary contexts. The heterogeneous nature of Indian folklore serves as a testament to the nation's pluralistic identity and its capacity to evolve with societal changes.

Folklore's influence in contemporaneity extends beyond preserving culture and providing entertainment as it now also serves as a cornerstone for modern narrative art. Analysis of various artistic mediums, including literature and film, demonstrates how contemporary creators draw inspiration from traditional tales, crafting innovative interpretations that resonate with today's audiences. The multiplicity and dynamic nature of folkloric narratives allows for its convergence with pressing issues like identity, gender, and social equity underscores its enduring relevance and catalyses critical societal discussions.

Essential to folklore is its ability to shape identities by rooting a community's existence and binding it with select narratives. This relationship between Indian folklore and identity formation highlights its significant role in shaping both individual and collective consciousness. The vibrant tapestry of cultural narratives, their inherent teachings, and their ongoing evolution—adapting to contemporary contexts while maintaining core values—merit academic investigation. This exploration not only deepens our understanding of cultural heritage but also encourages engagement in current debates on culture, narrative and identity within the Indian context. Moreover, it acts as a vital conduit for transmitting ethical principles, social norms, and historical accounts across the diverse Indian subcontinent. This vibrant oral tradition encapsulates society's philosophical and moral foundations, offering insights into the collective psyche that has influenced generations. Each narrative, imbued with metaphorical and allegorical elements, reflects the unique experiences of various communities, fostering a sense of identity and belonging while preserving the intricacies of local customs.

In a multicultural environment such as India, exposure to diverse regional narratives sharing common moral themes is a common experience. For instance, the tales of Akbar and Birbal not only entertain but also impart essential values such as wisdom, justice, and friendship— principles deeply ingrained in familial and social structures. Similar to these in every village and community would be such tales not yet brought to light, a few of which have been explored in the stories of this book.

Another significant essence of folklore lies in its function as a catalyst for community cohesion. Along with enabling within individual's a personal set of beliefs and shaping identity, it exemplifies how narratives can unify diverse groups to cultivate a collective identity. During festivals like Makar Sankranti, the recitation of local folklore engages participants and fosters connections among individuals from varied backgrounds. These celebrations feature stories of local deities and historical figures, serving as cultural signifiers that evoke pride and a shared heritage. Such occasions underscore the intricate relationship between folklore and community, highlighting its role as a unifying force in a society characterized by diversity.

The pervasive influence of Indian folklore on modern narratives is manifest across diverse artistic media. An analysis of contemporary literature and cinema unveils the ways in which folkloric components shape current storytelling techniques. Creative practitioners leverage mythological motifs and traditional narratives to confront present-day concerns, breathing new life into ancient tales while maintaining their pertinence to modern audiences. This dynamic interaction between traditional and contemporary elements exemplifies the fluidity of cultural expression and reaffirms the ongoing relevance of folklore as a vital touchstone for identity construction in Indian society.

A striking example of folklore's power in community settings occurred during a local event designed to educate and entertain children about their cultural heritage. An adept narrator recounted the story of a courageous village woman who challenged societal norms to protect her family from external dangers. The tale captivated listeners of all ages, each engrossed by the intricacies of her bravery. The story's immediate emotional impact was significant, not only conveying lessons of courage but also sparking discussions on gender roles in modern contexts. Her acts of valor became a cornerstone of collective identity, showcasing how folklore can energize social discourse and motivate future generations.

This profound connection with folklore continues to shape understanding of cultural significance, highlighting the lasting relevance of these narratives in cultivating moral comprehension and community bonds. The intricate relationship between folklore and identity drives academic interest in studying how historically-rooted tales mold and influence contemporary society. The rich array of narratives in Indian folklore presents a complex tapestry woven with threads of diverse cultural, linguistic, and geographical nuances. Each Indian region boasts a wealth of stories, from Rajasthan's vivid folk tales to Tamil Nadu's deep mythologies, illustrating how narrative forms and themes adapt to local contexts. These stories not only reflect distinct community identities but also illuminate universal human experiences, creating space for multifaceted interpretations of social emotions, relationships, and roles.

Regional narratives display significant variations in their treatment of common themes, offering valuable insights into the sociocultural fabric of their respective areas. For instance, Maharashtra's oral traditions use humor and satire to address the complexities of caste and social hierarchies, while Punjabi folklore often celebrates bravery and agricultural life, capturing the essence of its people. This diverse narrative landscape provides a rich foundation for examining how cultural practices and geographic influences shape perceptions of identity and belonging. An exploration of these folkloric accounts uncovers underlying lessons of resilience and adaptation in the face of adversity, which resonate with many individuals' experiences within these communities.

The multifaceted nature of Indian folklore reflects the pluralistic character of Indian society, encompassing numerous languages and dialects. Each linguistic group possesses its own body of myths and legends, contributing to a vast canon that honors the rich ethnic and cultural diversity. For example, the oral epics of the Northeast, such as those of the Apatani and Naga tribes, demonstrate profound connections with nature, spirituality, and community, contrasting sharply with the widely recognized Sanskrit epics like the Ramayana and Mahabharata, which permeate the country's literary landscape. These narratives function not only as entertainment but also as pedagogical tools, transmitting social values and norms across generations.

This remarkable diversity has profoundly influenced the understanding of the intricacies of Indian identity and narratives. Interaction with various folk narratives provides alternative perspectives on the construction, negotiation, and expression of identity within different cultural contexts. A dialogue emerges between stories that transcend linguistic boundaries, where themes of love, betrayal, hope, and heroism resonate irrespective of regional distinctions. In this realm, narratives become acts of resistance, with marginalized voices emerging through the reclamation of traditional tales, reasserting agency within an ever-evolving sociopolitical landscape.

A prime example of this phenomenon is the resurgence of mythological themes in mainstream cinema. Movies such as "Baahubali" and "Tumbbad" incorporate mythological frameworks and folkloric elements, skillfully blending them with modern cinematic techniques. In the literary sphere, a revival of folklore is evident in the works of authors like Arundhati Roy and Salman Rushdie, who interweave traditional motifs with contemporary themes. Digital storytelling platforms are no exception. Contemporary mediums such as web series and podcasts serve as innovative channels for age-old tales, allowing creators to reimagine folklore for modern audiences. The fusion of traditional and contemporary storytelling highlights the continued relevance of folklore as a vehicle for social and political commentary. The influence of folklore is also apparent in the visual arts domain. Contemporary artists often incorporate traditional motifs to explore themes of identity and cultural heritage. The integration of folk- art styles, such as Warli or Madhubani paintings, into modern artistic expressions demonstrates the enduring capacity of these historical art forms to convey current narratives, fostering discussions on identity, resistance, and community in our increasingly interconnected world.

Folklore, then, is not merely a historical artifact but a dynamic body of work crucial to comprehending the evolving mosaic of Indian culture and identity in the present day. The immersion in Indian folklore can be a transformative experience, offering insights that profoundly (re)shape personal identity and broaden one's worldview. Encountering the diverse narratives embedded in these traditional stories provides a unique perspective on the multifaceted cultural identities coexisting within India. Exposure to regional tales, each infused with local flavours and universal moral lessons, facilitates a deeper understanding of Indian cultural nuances, which are inextricably linked to values such as resilience, community, and reverence for nature.

The exploration of Indian folklore offers a profound examination of the human condition as expressed through these narratives. It also sheds light on the intricate interplay of identities within Indian society. The rich tapestry of languages, customs, and traditions woven into these narratives reflects India's multifaceted character. Each region's folkloric contributions add a unique thread to the national fabric, showcasing the country's pluralistic nature. Delving into stories from diverse communities, from the epic Ramayana to the folk songs of the Bhil tribe, cultivates a genuine appreciation for cultural diversity—a vital perspective in our increasingly homogeneous global environment.

This scholarly pursuit transcends academic boundaries, facilitating a deep reconnection with cultural roots. These folkloric tales engender a sense of belonging that extends beyond geographical confines. In an age of rapid globalization, where modern influences often eclipse traditional narratives, preserving these stories fosters a sense of grounding and continuity. This engagement strengthens one's Indian identity, serving as a bridge to ancestral wisdom and the lasting significance of communal ties.

Indian folklore should not be dismissed as an outdated relic. Instead, it represents a living narrative that continues to inspire and unify communities. Engaging with these stories instils a deep respect for cultural heritage and emphasizes the importance of its preservation for future generations. This awareness fuels a commitment to champion folklore's significance as a dynamic component of India's legacy, serving as a catalyst for both individual growth and community resilience.

Acknowledgement

This compilation of folktales is presented with profound appreciation for the invaluable support and contributions of everyone who made it possible. Dr. Deepti Pajni and Dr. Gitanjali Mahendra, and their guidance which was essential to the project's fruition. To Dr. Himanshu Parmar who deserves special recognition for cultivating a passion to explore beyond conventional narrative frameworks. Understanding that as folklores are repositories of cultural heritage and collective wisdom, this anthology strives to honor this cultural richness and disseminate it to a wider readership.

Sincere gratitude is extended to the narrators who shared their stories. Their voices, steeped in tradition and imbued with cultural significance constitute the essence of this collection. Each narrative reflects the intricacies of human experience, and the confidence placed in the conveyance of these tales is deeply valued.

Recognition is due to the final year students of B.A. English Honors (2022-2025) and M.A. English (2023-2025), whose meticulous research and perceptive analyses established the groundwork for comprehending these narratives. Their commitment to folklore studies has not only enhanced the selection process but also provided crucial analytical frameworks for appreciating each tale's significance within its cultural context.

Appreciation is also expressed to the publishing team, whose unwavering support and expertise transformed this anthology from concept to reality. Their dedication to quality and precision ensured the stories were presented with appropriate reverence.

Heartfelt gratitude is extended to the communities that have preserved their storytelling traditions. This anthology aspires to honour their legacies and inspire future generations to engage with their cultural narratives. Finally, recognition is given to the readers who engage with these folktales. Your interaction is vital; through your intellectual curiosity and imagination, you become part of the ongoing evolution of these narratives, bridging the past and the present.

Table of Contents

1. The Legend of Dayana Park 1
   Anchal

2. The Origin of Kullu Dussehra 5
   Aastha Awasthi

3. Twilight's Hush 8

4. Srinag Dhamuni and Mahunag 12
   Harshita Thakur

5. Khait Parvat: A Place Where Real Fairies Live...............15
   Garima Kathiyal

6. The Legacy of Hatkoti Temple 20
   Nikita Thakur

7. The Song of Gambhari Devi...24
   Shambhavi Sharma

8. Shiva Temple...27
   Shreya Thakur

9. Kunju Chanchalo 30
   Srishti Basnet

10	The Bear Tree 33
	Preksha Verma
11	Uncovering a Deity 38
	Samriti Sharma
12	Dhoban 40
	Akshita Chauhan
13	The Legend of the River and the Rose 45
	Devyani Pathania
14	The Curse of the Natvani 50
	Ayushi
15	The Ghost That Got Away 53
	Arushi Pathania
16	The Tragic Tale of Thakur Moni 58
	Shreya Mishra
17	The Legend of the Ban Jhakri 63
	Tanuja
18	Hadi Rani 67
	Varuna Rajvi
19	Whispers of the Lake 71
	Shruti
20	The Eternal Gurdians of the Western Himalayas 74
	Mehvish Sauhta
21	Hun Dass Chaukidara 83
	Mantasha Ansari

22	The Bride of Churdhar: A Tale of Lost Love .... 88 *Tanya Sharma*	
23	Rul Kul Devi .... 93 *Kanupriya*	
24	Rukmani Kund .... 98 *Divyanshi*	
25	Chaunidhar Shiva Temple .... 100 *Riya Verma*	
26	Quila Mubarak .... 105 *Achint Mann*	
27	Kali Bari Temple .... 107 *Zenab Ansari*	
28	Bijeshwar Devta Temple .... 111 *Smriti*	
29	The Tale of Dhola and Maru .... 114 *Ankita Sharma*	
30	Dhola Maru .... 118 *Disha Bahukhandi*	
31	The Story of Baz Bahadur and Roopmati .... 120 *Violet Mary George*	
32	The Unknown Encounter .... 123 *Ravinderpreet Kaur*	

The Legend of Dayana Park

Nestled in the verdant embrace of Ghogar Dhar, Dayana Park, also known as Dayana Baadh, stands as a testament to the rich tapestry of nature and folklore that defines the Mandi region of Himachal Pradesh, India. This hilltop station, celebrated for its breathtaking mountain-edge views and idyllic picnic spots, is equally renowned for its mystical narratives that have been woven into the cultural fabric of the local community. Among its many natural wonders, the park is home to an infamous upside-down tree, a peculiar botanical anomaly that has sparked a myriad of interpretations and tales, each adding to the park's enigmatic allure.

The upside-down tree, often viewed through the lens of superstition and folklore, serves as a focal point for both curiosity and reverence. Some locals regard it as a mystical entity, imbued with supernatural qualities, while others attribute its unusual appearance to a lightning strike that rendered its upper portion lifeless. This juxtaposition of natural phenomena and mythological interpretation exemplifies the broader narrative of Dayana Park, where the lines between reality and myth often blur, inviting visitors to ponder the mysteries that lie within.

One of the most captivating legends associated with Dayana Park is the tale of the eternal struggle between the Dayans, or witches, and the Hindu Gods, known as Devtas. This narrative, steeped in local tradition, posits that an annual confrontation occurs in the month of Kala Mahina, typically around mid-August. During this time, the park becomes a battleground for these supernatural entities, with the outcome of their clash believed to dictate the socio-economic and spiritual climate of the region for the ensuing year. The folklore suggests that the fight lasts for approximately seven to eight days, during which the gates of local temples remain closed, symbolizing the temporary withdrawal of divine protection.

The significance of this annual event transcends mere storytelling; it serves as a cultural ritual that shapes the behaviors and beliefs of the local populace. Residents are said to take specific precautions during this period, such as avoiding bright colors like red and yellow, which are thought to attract the attention of the witches. Additionally, many individuals engage in protective practices, such as encircling their homes with mustard seeds or carrying them in their pockets, believing these seeds to be talismans against malevolent forces. These customs highlight the community's deep-seated belief in the power of folklore to influence reality and underscore the lengths to which individuals will go to safeguard themselves during this time of perceived vulnerability.

The outcome of the witches' and Gods' battle is believed to be indicative of the prosperity and harmony that will prevail in the region for the year ahead. If the weather remains clear during the fight, it is interpreted as a sign that the witches have triumphed, often leading to a year marked by misfortune, loss of life, and property. Conversely, if storms and rain accompany the clash, it is seen as a victory for the Gods, heralding a season of agricultural abundance and peace.

The final verdict of this mythical contest is traditionally announced by a figure known as Dev Vanni, who interprets the signs and conditions prevailing throughout the year to declare the victors. In contemporary times, the results of this age-old struggle have found their way into newspapers and social media platforms, bridging the gap between ancient tradition and modern communication.

The tale of Dayana Park, with its intertwining of nature, folklore, and community practices, has transcended the confines of Mandi, spreading far beyond its geographical boundaries. For thousands of years, the narrative has been passed down through generations, with each retelling serving to reinforce the cultural identity of the region. The enduring belief in the witches and Gods, and the rituals associated with their annual confrontation, continue to resonate with both locals and visitors alike, fostering a sense of connection to the land and its storied past. Dayana Park stands not only as a natural wonder but also as a cultural landmark steeped in folklore that reflects the beliefs and values of the Mandi community. The interplay of nature and myth at this site invites contemplation and exploration, drawing individuals into a world where the supernatural and the natural coexist harmoniously. As the annual battle between the Dayans and the Devtas unfolds, it serves as a poignant reminder of the power of storytelling in shaping human experience and the enduring legacy of cultural traditions that continue to thrive in the face of modernity. Thus, Dayana Park remains a mystical enclave, where the echoes of ancient tales reverberate through the valleys, captivating the hearts and minds of all who venture into its embrace.

Source: The tale is narrated by the villagers of Ghogar Dhar.

The Origin of Kullu Dussehra

The Kullu valley, situated within the Himalayan landscape, stands as a living repository of time-honored traditions, customs, and folkloric narratives. Among the region's rich tapestry of tales, one recounts the origins of Kullu Dussehra, a festival intrinsically connected to the historical figure of Kullu Jagat Singh, a former ruler. This annual celebration, marked by its passionate observance, exemplifies the enduring cultural legacy and oral traditions that have persisted through successive generations. In contemporary times, the Dussehra festival remains a vibrant and integral component of the community's cultural fabric, serving as a unifying event that brings together diverse individuals in a collective commemoration of the perennial conflict between benevolence and malevolence. During ancient times, a modest Brahmin maintained a strong rapport with the sovereign, regularly offering advice. This intimate alliance stirred resentment among fellow advisors, who conspired against the Brahmin. They circulated a fictitious tale about his ownership of "sucche moti" (authentic pearls) and convinced the ruler that these valuable gems should be considered royal property by decree.

Influenced by the misleading information, the king ordered the Brahmin to surrender the pearls. The Brahmin vehemently denied possession, but the monarch remained skeptical and even dispatched his representatives to pressure him. As a last resort, the ruler declared his impending journey and demanded that the pearls be delivered upon his homecoming, warning of severe consequences if his commands were not heeded.

Faced with unjust accusations and impending punishment, the Brahmin, in a state of utter despair, imprisoned his family within their dwelling and ignited it. Upon the monarch's return, the Brahmin, in a final act of tragic rebellion, began dismembering himself and casting the pieces into the inferno, exclaiming, "Le raja, tere sucche moti" (Here, king, take your precious jewels). This horrific spectacle invoked a curse upon the ruler, afflicting him with "kusht rog" (leprosy), as he had perpetrated the transgression of "Brahm dosh" by wronging a Brahmin. The malady commenced its spread from the sovereign's hands, gradually engulfing the rest of his body.

Faced with a dire situation, the sovereign consulted the religious authorities for counsel. They revealed that the sole means of redemption for his wrongdoing and elimination of the plague was to acquire the effigy of Lord Raghunath from Ayodhya. Subsequently, the ruler dispatched a pair of trustworthy emissaries well-versed in the arcane art of "Gutika Siddhi," an ability that allowed them to dematerialize and traverse extensive distances swiftly.

The individuals spent two years in Ayodhya, acquiring knowledge of the correct rituals for idol veneration. However, their return journey with the idol was impeded by Ayodhya's clergy, who refused to allow their departure. As the priests attempted to restore the idol to its original location, they were suddenly afflicted with blindness. Intriguingly, their vision was restored when they oriented themselves towards Kullu. This phenomenon was interpreted as a divine indication that Lord Raghunath intended to establish himself in Kullu.

Upon retrieving the idol, the monarch's soldiers brought it back, and the ruler ceremoniously placed it in Kullu with utmost respect. He proclaimed Lord Raghunath as the presiding deity of the area. This act of worship and atonement not only healed the king's ailment but also initiated Kullu's profound connection with Lord Raghunath. This relationship ultimately led to the establishment of the grand Dussehra celebration, which continues to honor the deity to this day.

Source: Spoken legends shared by the populace of the Kullu district.

Twilight's Hush

For centuries whispers of a tale have remained, reverberating as echoes in the ears of villagers. It emerges from the mists and drowns with the sunset, like the human's wish for a companion. A need to find someone within life's darkness, one to share all the simplicities of the daily life.

The story begins back in the days, in a haven of tranquility far from the city's sight. Unspoiled and authentic. The twilight always brought more than just darkness with itself and lived its fullest before the dawn. The houses in Mahavan seemed to grow from earth and the forest combined, etched in the mud and gentle embrace of wood. The muddy walls and wooden floors always preserved some secrets. One among the many secrets which it carried were those of a man and his wife who had been living in the village of Mahavan at the top of Dhar.

Their house, although a little isolated from the rest of the village, was a part of the same little hamlet. The little house with only one room had a set of frail wooden stairs leading up to the attic which was their rasoi. The mornings would be filled with applying a fresh layer of a muddy mixture all over the mud walls giving the whole house a new appearance and fading the dark parched cracks near the chulha. Rest of the morning rituals would be the same everyday, where the wife would burn wood under the brass vessel polished with a thick paste of wooden ashes. The heated apricot oil in the vessel would soon fill the air with its light scent which would then wake the sleeping man in the room below it. The wooden floor squeaked every time he'd make his way outside the door to bath, signaling the wife that her husband has awoken. Though married life was not amorous, they were accustomed to their roles and responsibilities, and with no one else in the family, the meal hours would witness just two steel plates near the rugs made of the old torn clothes sewn together.

One day, when dawn brought with itself the demise of his wife, the man was left with the painful thoughts of spending the remaining days of his life all alone. After the end of the rituals, he returned home to complete silence. The room never felt emptier. Making his way up to the attic which was filled with the saturated hue of the sunset, he made the decision of bringing her back. From what he had always heard about the dead, he knew that the spirit of the dead comes to visit the sacred temple of their deity which was located at the top of the Dhar. Then, at the crematory a ceremonious celebration would take place with the other spirits whose mortal bodies were burnt at the same place to celebrate the arrival of a new spirit. While the whole village would be sound asleep, he knew, in the realms of darkness as the spirits of the past came alive and so shall his wife that night.

He decided to grab the opportunity to sneak in on their unearthly celebration and look for his wife the same night. He visited the crematory and hide behind the bushes to pry into a different realm. He soon was surrounded by sinister sounds and after finally resting his eyes upon a bunch of blear bodies dancing near the cold ashes of his wife. He soon recognized his wife among them. In the fear of not ever finding her again, he considered the moment to be the perfect opportunity to bring her back. He unveiled his identity and grabbed her hand to drag her along with him back home. She felt real. Ignoring what she had become now, he was successful in bringing her back.

There was no word heard from her mouth ever since for she had changed. A mere wisp of what she once was, now she would only engage herself with roasting mouli (dried seeds and nuts) on a big black iron tawa burning on top of the flaming hot hearth. She had a brush made up of slender dried pine needles which were held together in place with a small rope tied at the top. With this she'd glide the mouli back and forth. These were commonly eaten in every house in the village especially during the winters to keep the body warm or as a snack. The husband made several attempts to talk to her hut she'd never reply, nor initiate conversation. She kept herself engaged in roasting the mouli.

After days full of uncountable failed attempts, the husband decided to hide the brush so that his wife would talk to him, even if it was merely to ask about the brush. He kept waiting in the room below, for her to come down from the attic, looking for the brush, but the whole day passed by. After waiting he climbed up the stairs to the attic, where he could not find his wife. All there was in the attic was a dying flame in the heart running out of wood and a plate full of mouli near the rug. His attempt to revitalize her along with his life, failed. Having realized that he could not find her now, he pictured her sitting near the chulha one last time and then gave a hopeless glance at the brush in his hand.

According to some villagers, they were blessed with children before the death of the wife but the evidence is limited. The man's attempt to defy the order of life and death failed, leaving him with a deeper understanding of the impermanence of life.

Srinag Dhamuni and Mahunag

Srinag Dhamuni or Naag Dhamuni temple is situated at Dhamun valley in Seri Banglo and Sainj Bangra, Karsog. It is 3000 years old, situated at 22000 ft. approx height. Whereas Mahunag Temple is set in the village of Bakhari in the same Karsog valley. It is set at a striking elevation of 1830-2000 m above sea level overlooking the valley. There are several legends and tales surrounding the two devtas popular in the region.

The Mahunag temple is dedicated to Mahunag, who is believed to be an avatar of Karna from the Hindu epic Mahabharata. The Mahunag temple was built in the 17th century by Raja Shyam Sen and the idol of Karna was brought and worshipped on his birthday for the first time. The story behind the deity dates to ancient times when it is believed a farmer, while tilling his land uncovered the makhota of the deity. The devta spoke to him, informing him that he is a Nag and is called Mahunag. Later, it was when Raja Shyam Sen was once imprisoned by the Mughal emperor in Delhi that he prayed for divine help. It is believed that Mahunag, hearing his plea, appeared inside the jail cell in the form of a mahu (bee) and helped set him free. For saving his life, the king promised half his kingdom to the devta and vowed to celebrate and honor his divine presence each year by organizing an annual fair which is held in the month of July.

Nag devta Dhamuni is at the same time believed to be Mahabharata's Arjun. Interestingly, while both the devtas are worshipped in the form of Nag, Mahunag is revered for his power to cure snakebites.

One of the many stories of the two devtas is recounted by the people of Karsog valley:

Once Mahung and Dhamuni were having a conversation about the height of their peaks and how tall one's mountain is from the other. Dhamuni, being a little roguish proposed a competition with Mahunag which stated that both of them would destroy their mountain to the last bit at the bottom and then grow it again from scratch. This would allow them to start anew and determine which mountain would stand taller.

Mahunag, considering it to be a fair competition, razed his mountain peak causing complete mayhem. Dhamuni on the other hand brought a thick fog all over the place making it unclear for Mahunag to see any bit of Dhamuni's mountain. To mimic the sound of crashing rocks and stones, Dhamuni dropped apricots off from some of the trees. This was done to make it appear that Dhamuni was as per their pact destroying his mountain.

After some time when the fog was cleared Mahunag was furious to see Dhamuni's mountain untouched while his own mountain was nothing but dust and rubble.

Hence, this is believed that this is the reason that the Dhamuni's temple is at a higher level than Mahunag's temple. Some even believe that these two devtas still continue to harbor rivalry with each other. People also draw parallels between them by relating it to the relationship shared by Karna and Arjuna throughout the Mahabharata.

Ever since, the mountains remain as a lasting reminder of the enduring power of competition and the eternal rivalrous spirit of these two devtas.

Source: A Spoken Folklore circulated among residents of Karsog, Lahri and Dhadaun Settlements.

Khait Parvat: A Place Where Real Fairies Live

Nestled in the serene, undulating landscapes of the Tehri district of Uttarakhand, India, lies a mountain steeped in mystery and folklore, Khait Parvat. Often overlooked by mainstream tourism, this enchanting locale has a captivating allure, not only due to its breathtaking natural beauty but also because of the local legends that speak of otherworldly beings known as "aanchri" or "bharadi." According to the folklore of this region, these ethereal spirits, which are believed to be nine sisters, inhabit the mountain's nine distinct peaks. They are regarded as guardians of nearby villages, intertwined with extraordinary phenomena and apparitions that inspire both reverence and intrigue.

A compelling narrative that enriches the cultural tapestry of Khait Parvat revolves around the King of Tehri Garhwal, who is said to have resided there for some time. During his stay, he was graciously cared for by a local woman, Deepa Pawar. When Deepa inquired about the reason for the king's visit, he expressed his desire to marry her younger sister Deva. This revelation brought immense joy to the community, culminating in a royal wedding that intertwined their lives with their destiny. Soon after, the king married Deva, who later ascended the throne of Tehri Garhwal, and blessed with nine extraordinarily beautiful daughters..

As the daughters reached the age of 12, each girl began to dream of marrying six nagrajas or serpent kings. The following morning, the skies darkened ominously, except for the radiant peak of the Khait Parvat, which remained illuminated by sunlight. Inspired by this miraculous phenomenon, sisters ascended the mountain in search of clarity and brilliance. Upon reaching the summit, a transformative event transpired: they were said to have been miraculously converted into fairies. It is believed that these ethereal beings still reside on the mountain, safeguarding their surroundings and enriching the folklore that continues to capture the hearts of locals and visitors alike.

The unique environmental conditions of Khait Parvat contribute significantly to its mystique. The mountain appears to defy nature, exhibiting unexplained phenomena, such as the spontaneous growth of apricot trees and garlic without human intervention. Furthermore, the flora remains lush and prosperous, with trees that bear fruit year-round, providing sustenance and a striking contrast to the rugged terrain surrounding them.

Khait Parvat is also home to an impressive array of rare floral species that enhance its scenic charm, making it an extraordinary destination for natural enthusiasts and botanists. Such extraordinary natural occurrences fuel local speculation, prompting some to wonder if these phenomena are indeed influenced by the fairies that are said to inhabit the mountain.

The Mystery of Caves:

Among the enduring enigmas of Khait, Parvat is a deep cave whose extensive length remains largely unexplored.

Within this cave, peculiar drawings of snakes have been discovered, symbols steeped in significance within Hindu mythology, where snakes are often associated with Lord Shiva, the deity of destruction and transformation. Such artifacts deepen the intrigue surrounding the mountain and prompt ongoing discussions on its cultural and spiritual importance. Local residents claimed to witness fairies dancing atop the mountain, surrounded by a surreal and otherworldly atmosphere. Reports of laughter and jubilant music echoing through the forests add to the tapestry of enchantments woven around Khait Parvat. Some individuals have even described the experiences of being momentarily possessed by these beings, only to return after days with no recollection of their time spent in the fairies' realm.

The Story of Jeetu Bagdwal:

One particularly famous tale associated with Khait Parvat involves a local named Jeetu Bagdwal, whose flute melodies are said to have mesmerized fairies residing in the mountain. Captivated by his enchanting music, the fairies are believed to have descended and taken Jeetu into their mystical domains. The locals maintain that even after his disappearance, Jeetu continues to watch over his family and community from within the mountain, earning deep respect and reverence from the villagers who still worship him as a protector.

An annual fair is held in Khait in June, attracting not only local villagers but also visitors from around the world. However, the villagers of Khait have implemented specific rules for the fair, including prohibitions against loud shouting, playing loud music, and wearing bright colors. These restrictions are based on the belief that such activities may attract the attention of fairies who are said to reside on the mountain, potentially leading to the abduction of humans, as in the case of Jeetu Bagdwal. While the existence of fairies remains a matter of belief, the legends surrounding the khait parvat offer a glimpse of the rich cultural heritage of the region.

Khait Parvat is more than just a striking geographical feature; it is a living repository of myths, culture, and the natural world, where the lines between reality and folklore blur into one another. Whether drawn by the stories of nine fairy sisters, captivated by the enchanting melodies of flute music, or simply seeking solace in nature, Khait Parvat offers a unique experience encapsulated in mystery and beauty. This remote paradise reminds us of the legends that shape our understanding of the world, urging us to explore the unseen dimensions that coexist with reality. As the whispers of fairies dance on the mountain breeze, one cannot help but feel a sense of enchantment and wonder in this place, where real fairies are believed to dwell.

Source: Traditional songs and tales shared by residents of the region.

The Legacy of Hatkoti Temple

The serene hamlet of Kharshaali, located in the Himachal Pradesh highlands, housed a venerated shrine dedicated to a Goddess. This devi was associated with conferring tranquility and affluence upon her adherents. Notably, this regional patroness was also characterized by her formidable disposition. Initially modest and devout, the local populace experienced a period of prosperity, ostensibly attributed to her beneficence, spanning several years. Nevertheless, as temporal progression ensued and the community's economic status improved, individuals from external regions began to cultivate sentiments of antipathy towards the denizens of Kharshaali.

Once this happened, a drought hit all villages in the region. The impact was massive as crops failed and famine spread across the region. Villagers desperate to save their lands turned to dark traditions to bring Kharshali to ruins. The elders advised that a sacrifice must be offered to the goddess to end the drought. Hearing this, the people envious of the prospering village of Kharshaali hatched a plan to get rid of both the famine and prosperity of Kharshaali. They suggested that a human be sacrificed so that the Goddess would be more pleased with the devotion of the villagers.

Thus, the search began to look for a suitable person to sacrifice. After many unsuccessful attempts, a scapegoat in the form of a young gorkha (a man of Nepali origin), who was dumb and poor, was found. This man had come to Kharshaali, looking for work to earn a living. Not only was he unable to speak, but he also had no family in the region and was often found wandering the village, picking any job that was given to him by the villagers. His silence made him an easy target for evil villagers. Keeping this in mind, one of the villagers suggested that this man should be presented as a sacrifice before the Goddess to seek her blessings and end the long spell of drought.

No one questioned the decision, for they feared the long-term effects of the drought and were desperately looking for a solution. Hence, the villagers agreed that the man would be tied up and prepared for sacrifice. They hoped that by offering the life of this man, the Goddess would be pleased, and the drought would come to end. Thus, everyone stood silent to watch the ritual performed. No single person spoke against it.

However, unbeknownst to the villagers, the Goddess, who had always watched Kharshaali with a loving eye, saw what was happening. Her heart was filled with fury, as she saw the cruelty and ignorance of her own devotees. The Goddess was known to be a protector of the weak and innocent and she could not bear the thought of her followers taking the life of an innocent man, especially someone who could not even defend himself.

With a powerful gust of wind and a blinding flash of lightning, the earth trembled and the skies grew dark. The Goddess, in her wrath, appeared before the villagers.

Her eyes glared like burning coals, her voice thundered through the skies, and her divine presence shook the ground beneath their feet.

"You dare to take an innocent life to appease me?" she cried. "I am the protector of the weak, and I demand justice, not bloodshed. You have forgotten the true meaning of devotion." The villagers were struck by terror as they looked upon the wrathful Goddess. Their faces turned pale and the bonds around the man's wrists fell apart as the Goddess's anger swirled around them.

The goddess in her fury declared that she could no longer remain in Kharshaali. "This place is no longer worthy of my presence," she said. "Until you understand the value of life and the true meaning of devotion, I will leave this place." With the final roar, a flash of lightning, the goddess disappeared into a flood of water that broke through the mountains. She never returned to Kharshaali. The mute man, spared by the Goddess's mercy, fearfully fled the village. He wandered for days, eventually finding his way to Hatkoti. Here, the villagers heard of the terrible wrath of the Goddess and knew that only sincere devotion could restore her blessings. When the man arrived at the village, they took him in, fed him, and offered him their hospitality, seeing his innocence and understanding that life must be cherished and not taken.

As people of Hatkoti learned of the Goddess's wrath in Kharshaali, they gathered in prayer and promised to honor her with true devotion. Another gust of water brought onto the banks of the river, the Goddess, who had abandoned Kharshaali, gracing the village with her divine presence. They built a temple to the Goddess, henceforth calling her Hateshwari and celebrating her presence with reverence and respect. The rain returned, and the land flourished as her blessings graced Hatkoti. From that day forward, devi Hateshwari took her permanent residence in Hatkoti, where the villagers vowed never to forget the value of compassion and sanctity of life.

The narrative of Kharshaali serves as a poignant illustration that even the most formidable divine entity would not countenance brutality committed in her honor, and that authentic reverence necessitates compassion, esteem, and empathy. The deity's metamorphosis from Kharshaali to Hatkoti became an enduring mythos transmitted across generations, encapsulating a narrative of celestial wrath and clemency, while imparting a profound lesson on the sanctity of all existence.

Source: Mr. Sam Nath Dogra, a pharmacist in the Ayurvedic department, and other local people in Rohru.

The Song of Gambhari Devi

Gambhari Devi (1992-2013) was a veteran Indian Folk singer, folklorist and dancer from Kehloor, (now known as district Bilaspur) of Himachal Pradesh. One of her famous folk songs is "KAHANA PEENA NAND LENE O GAMBHARIYE." That simply means eat, drink and enjoy

Gambhari Devi, a talented folk performer, embodied the spirit of her village through her songs, dances, and stories. Despite the challenging terrain and isolation of her mountainous home, she found inspiration in her surroundings, transforming her experiences into melodies that captured both life's simple pleasures and profound hardships. One twilight, as the setting sun bathed the terraced landscape in a golden light, Gambhari joined a gathering of villagers around a fire. The crisp air carried the pulsating rhythms of the dholak, drawing everyone to listen and experience the moment. The villagers had assembled, anticipating her performance. It was a rare instance when daily worries seemed to fade away temporarily.

As Gambhari Devi's voice rose, reminiscent of a gentle mountain breeze, she began her song, "Kahana Peena Nand Lene O Gambhariye." The lyrics, though simple, carried deep wisdom: "Eat, drink, and enjoy, Gambhariye." This wasn't merely an invitation to celebrate; it was an encouragement to embrace life fully, to cease fretting over unchangeable difficulties, and to appreciate life's small blessings. The villagers listened attentively, relating to the message. Mountain life was challenging, with limited access to nearby towns, but the residents of Bandla persevered with quiet strength. They cherished their livestock like family and found happiness in modest pleasures, such as communal meals or scenic sunsets.

Gambhari's song resonated with them, celebrating not grand accomplishments, but everyday gratitude. Through her lyrics, she personified the Bandla hills, highlighting their rugged beauty that only locals could truly appreciate. She likened her village to "the moon among the stars," emphasizing its unique charm and subtle grace. Her words echoed a sentiment familiar to the villagers: beauty lies in the eye of the beholder. To them, their homeland was as precious as any urban center or royal residence because it was their own. As the dholak's tempo increased, Gambhari's voice grew more powerful. She encouraged the villagers to immerse themselves in the music, to dance, and to momentarily forget their troubles. She reminded them of life's brevity and the futility of excessive worry. She urged them to treasure their blessings – the joy of children's laughter, the comfort of home, the companionship of animals, and the beauty of the hills that cradled them. As the song came to an end, the fire crackled, and the villagers sat in quiet reflection. Gambhari Devi smiled, knowing that through her music, she had reminded them of something vital. Life wasn't about chasing after distant dreams or dwelling on past regrets. It was about living fully, appreciating what you had, and finding joy in the simplest things. In a world where women were often silenced and their contributions overlooked, Gambhari Devi had carved out a space for herself and her people. Her songs, rich with the rhythms of her land, would live on in the hearts of all who heard them. And for the villagers of Bandla, her music would always be a reminder to dance with life, even in its hardest moments. As the night grew darker, and the last of the stars blinked into view, the villagers left, carrying the music of Gambhari Devi in their hearts, knowing that tomorrow, they would rise again, ready to live fully, as she had taught them.

Source: Regional ballads and narratives shared by community members

Shiva Temple

Among the 84 parganas of the Chamba principality, Himgiri stands out as the most productive region. This area boasts extensive woodlands, with deodar trees covering roughly 40% of the land. The pargana features numerous settlements, both large and small, nestled among thriving crops and verdant orchards in the mountain range's lower slopes.

Himgiri pargana shares borders with Bhanauta pargana on one side and Diur pargana on the other. The Siul River forms from the water gathered from the entire Churah village, downstream from Chetri village. During the era of princely rule, Himgiri earned the moniker 'Annadaata' (meaning 'food grain donor') of Chamba, owing to its resilience against droughts and floods. Even in the 1980s, inhabitants of the Pangi valley would purchase grains from Himgiri, transporting them back on sheep.

In mythology, Himgiri was referred to as 'Shail Rajya,' and Shailja, the daughter of Shail, was wedded to Lord Shiva, who resides on Mount Kailash. Legend has it that the Pandavas spent their final year of exile in hiding within Himgiri, following their twelve-year banishment. Consequently, numerous Pandava-related memories are linked to this region.

The village of Shamwai houses a remarkable Shiva temple. According to local lore, the Pandavas constructed this temple during their 'Agyaatvaas' (period of anonymity). The temple's massive stone blocks, several feet in height and width, are beyond the capabilities of ordinary individuals to carve or assemble. Similar enormous carved stones can be found scattered throughout Shamwai's fields, suggesting that the entire village and its surroundings once formed a vast temple complex.

Raja Shri Singh was once held captive in Lahore jail. It is said that Lord Shiva appeared to him in a dream, instructing him to install roofs on the temples in Bhadarwah and Shamwai. Upon his release, the Raja personally visited Bhadarwah and dispatched his minister to oversee the roof construction at Shamwai temple. Despite Bagha Wazir's numerous attempts, the temple roof repeatedly collapsed. Legend has it that Shiva's spirit descended upon a follower, informing the minister that only by sacrificing two daughters in the temple's inner sanctum could the roof be successfully built.

Bagha Wazir approached a man of the Bhat caste from nearby Kahlog village and convinced him to sell his two daughters. One girl, purchased for 100 rupees, was named Shambi, after whom Shamwai village was named. The second, bought for 50 rupees, was called Panji, giving rise to the name Panjhei. The minister had both girls adorned and buried alive in the temple's inner sanctum, enabling the construction of the Shiva temple's roof. Additionally, the Naga culture in Chamba is said to have originated from Anjani Dal lake in Himgiri, which is another distinct historical narrative.

Another popular legend tells of a man named Sadh from Katoga village who experienced a strange phenomenon while returning home. As he reached Dehrighat ridge, he noticed darkness ahead but sunlight behind him. Confused, he turned back and encountered a human-like statue of Shakti Devi. Upon worshipping and lifting the statue, his path home became illuminated. Sadh brought the goddess statue to his house and installed it with proper rituals. Soon after, the area was terrorized by a tiger that killed seven people. Various locations were named after the tiger's victims: Gujjar-phati, where a Gujjar was attacked; Punni-phati, where a woman named Punni was killed; and Luhareri-phati, where a blacksmith was bitten. Frightened residents gathered in Katoga, seeking protection from Shakti Devi. The goddess's shadow appeared to her disciple, assuring the people that the tiger would cease its attacks if they built a temple at Dehrighat and held an annual Jatar (fair). This marked the beginning of the Dehrighat Jatar tradition.

Following Sadh's death, villagers moved the goddess idol to Kumda village. From there, the Shakti Devi idol was adorned with jewelry and garlands for the Dehrighat Jatar. This event has since become one of the most renowned fairs in the Churah valley.

Source: Translated from "CHURAH GHATI: EK PARICHAY" by DS Deval.

Kunju Chanchalo

Himachal Pradesh evokes images of towering peaks, verdant forests, cerulean skies, meandering roads, pine-lined paths, turbulent streams, and the genuine smiles of its residents. Having been raised in this region, I was enveloped by Himachal's awe-inspiring vistas, the valley's allure, the vibrant Himachali traditions, and the oral narratives and melodies that chronicled the lives of Gaddis, paramours, matriarchs, and siblings who called this land home. Regrettably, these oral traditions have gradually diminished over the years.

I am transcribing a folk ballad from Chamba that narrates the heartrending romance between Kunju, a Gaddi (shepherd) youth of low social standing, and Chanchalo, a maiden from an elevated caste. Their story exemplifies a love that is unadulterated, genuine, and exquisite. Chanchalo was also pursued by two other suitors: the monarch and his advisor. Owing to Kunju's inferior social status, the couple encountered numerous hardships, yet their devotion remained unfaltering, and they stood prepared to relinquish everything for one another.

Both the king and the minister were jealous of Kunju and Chanchalo's relationship. Since the king desired Chanchalo, the minister could not express his desire for her. However, his desire was more than that of a loser's sigh, and it turned into a devious move. The Minister approached the king with an idea. He told the king that Kunju that shepherd boys should be sent to war as they needed man for the battle and by doing the same, the lovers would not be able to meet each other. The King liked this idea. He was also childless, so he considered it his right to make Chanchalo his new queen. The news was sent to him, and Kunju knew he had to be dutiful, even though his heart was breaking at the thought of being separated from his beloved. He went to war with tearful eyes and heavy hearts.

The news shattered Chanchalo, yet her devotion remained steadfast. She was prepared to endure hardship for the sake of her affection. No challenge seemed beyond her capacity to overcome. In her nightly reveries, she encountered a tearful Kunju, their mutual adoration persisting within. Her yearning for her beloved evolved into a constant presence. She dedicated each day and night to beseeching for their eventual reunion. Meanwhile, on the distant battlefield, Kunju shared this aspiration, longing for the moment he could return to his cherished abode and reunite with his dear Chanchalo.

Meanwhile, the king and minister were elated, thinking that they had managed to separate the lovers. The king himself, under the influence of his cunning minister, took some very bad decisions for his kingdom, which was later revealed as the minister was the man of ill thoughts for others.

Days passed until a messenger arrived in the beautiful valley with devestating news. Kunju had been killed. On the battlefield, while fighting for the kingdom, he was tricked and slaughtered.

Upon hearing of his death, Chanchalo was inconsolable, the pain was unbearable, and with the thought of reuniting with her beloved, she decided to end her mortal life. Knowing the king's decision and the minister's evil intentions and blaming them to send off her beloved to die, she cursed the two to a death devoid of love and honor. She then took her life.

When the king heard the news, he was filled with remorse, and in repentance, he committed suicide. The minister glad to have ridded himself off the lovers, and the king slept unbothered in bed, where he was murdered by a thief. The story and its tragic end have been preserved in the folk tradition of the Chamba district of Himachal Pradesh. Keeping preserved the memory of the lovers forever it's become one of the famous folktales of the Chamba region

A folktale, deeply rooted in the traditions of Chamba, was relayed to me by my cousin who hails from that region. This particular narrative, which forms part of the area's cultural heritage, had been transmitted to him by his grandmother, preserving the oral tradition across generations.

Source: Cousin who heard the story from his grandmother.

The Bear Tree

Nestled in the lap of the Himalayas, Himachal Pradesh is a burgeoning land of exquisite natural beauty, with majestic mountains, lush valleys, and serene lakes. However, what truly sets this state apart is its spiritual heritage, often referred to as 'Devbhoomi' or 'Land of Gods.' This appellation is not merely ceremonial, but is a reflection of the deep spiritual and cultural fabric that defines the lives of its inhabitants. With a rich history of devotion, the state is home to numerous deities known locally as Devi Devtas, who are believed to provide protection and blessings to their devotees.

The Spiritual Tapestry of Himachal Pradesh

The heart of Himachal Pradesh is encapsulated in a multitude of deities, each revering in different regions and communities. From bustling towns to remote villages, diverse rituals and traditions embody the local populace's reverence towards their gods and goddesses. Worship practices vary, symbolizing the rich tapestry of beliefs that characterize the state, but the common thread is a profound faith that these divine beings shield them from harm and evil.

The inhabitants take their spirituality seriously and conduct rituals, festivals, and ceremonies throughout the year. These practices are not just acts of worship, but are essential elements of community bonding, where collective prayers and offerings are made to seek divine intervention in daily life trials.

The Tale of the Mendicant and the Goddess Pathri

One of the compelling stories that epitomizes the divine intervention reverberating in the hearts of the locals is that of a mendicant from Junga village near Shimla. The mendicant was known for his unwavering dedication, spending his days in deep meditation, and seemingly detached from the bustling life of the villagers around him. Despite the intrigue regarding his solitary existence, he remains a figure of mystery, captivating the minds of those who passed by.

The turning point in his story came during a torrential downpour that threatened to flood the village. While the rain inundated the land, an astonishing spectacle unfolded — the area around the mendicant remained remarkably dry, untouched by even a single drop of rain. It piqued the curiosity of the village king, who approached the mendicant with a mix of awe and concerns.

"Who are you? How can I serve you?" the king inquired. The mendicant, with a serene smile, revealed that he was the earthly embodiment of devotion to a goddess residing in the land they tread. He implored the king and villagers to worship this formidable goddess, promising divine protection from life's myriad peril.

In an age when belief in the divine could shift the course of life, villagers responded wholeheartedly. They constructed a temple dedicated to the Goddess Pathri Devi on the mountaintop, marking the inception of a long-standing veneration that continues to thrive.

Legendary Protection of Goddess Pathri

Goddess Pathri's legend, along with her protective powers, became the bedrock of community life in and around Junga. One such instance is etched in the memories of the villagers— the tale of a man who ventured into the nearby wilderness to gather grass for his animals. His innocent task was interrupted when a bear, a major yet fearsome animal, set its sights on him, instigating a frantic chase through the dense forest.

Fearing for his life, the man clawed his way up a towering Deodar tree, his heart racing as the bear followed suit, intent to claim its prey. With nowhere left to turn, the man lifted his voice in desperation, calling on Goddess Pathri to save him at his moment of peril. His fervent prayers were met with an extraordinary spectacle: the bear began to transform before his eyes and its form morphed into an inert piece of wood. What was once a ravenous predator was now an eternal testament to the power of faith lifelessly suspended on the branch of the tree.

To this day, that tree remains a historical site in Junga, adorned with the wooden representation of the bear, which now serves as a reminder of both the sheer power of devotion and divine protection. The temple of the Goddess Pathri stands as a testament to years of unwavering faith, attracting locals and tourists who come to pay their respect and offerings.

The tale of the Goddess Pathri and the mendicant embodies the ethos of Himachal Pradesh, a state where spirituality intertwines with everyday life. The annual rituals, festivals, and gatherings that congregate around this belief system are filled with color, music, and an undying spirit of faith that permeates the atmosphere. Whether it is a humble gathering of villagers or a grand festival involving thousands, the reverence of the divine is palpable and serves to strengthen communal ties.

The temple of the Goddess Pathri continuously echoes the prayers of devotees, who seek blessings not just for themselves, but also for the well-being of their families and community. The faith in the goddess is unwavering, with locals recounting miraculous events that reaffirm their belief in their protective grace.

Himachal Pradesh undeniably offers more than just an enchanting landscape; it is a reservoir for spirituality, culture, and history. The tales of deities like Goddess Pathri illustrate the bonds of faith that last through generations, guarding and guiding the lives of those who venerate them. In an age characterized by chaos and uncertainty, places such as Himachal Pradesh remind us of the enduring power of faith and the harmony it can bring to our lives.

As one explores the lush valleys and rocky hills of Himachal Pradesh, it's essential to acknowledge that behind every serene face rests a legacy of devotion that transcends time and geography. Each prayer, each offering, each festival contributes to an assurance that while dangers may lurk, the divine presence remains steadfast, forever watching over a land truly worthy of its designation as 'Devbhoomi.'

Source: Narrated by local people of the area.

Uncovering a Deity

According to a tale passed down by older generations, a shepherd once led his flock from the town of Rohru to the high-altitude pastures of Janglikh during the summer months. As the herd ventured deeper into the valley, the shepherd established a base camp in the vast meadow of Litham.

Typically, the sheep would roam and feed throughout the day, returning by nightfall. However, one evening, a few sheep failed to come back. The following morning, the shepherd embarked on a search, reaching Chandernahan lake. Despite days of searching, he couldn't locate the missing animals. Disheartened, he pressed on until he reached the seventh lake of Chandernahan, where he began playing his flute in despair.

Suddenly, a saint emerged from the lake's sacred waters, inquiring about the shepherd's distress. The shepherd explained his predicament, mentioning his missing sheep and his inability to return to camp due to the worsening weather. He also expressed concern about his wife worrying at home.

Moved by the shepherd's plight, the deity requested his flute as proof of his survival for his family. The shepherd respectfully complied, handing over the instrument.

Legend has it that miraculously, the shepherd's flute, after flowing downstream, reversed course and traveled upstream at the confluence of the Pabbar River and its tributary, Shikdi.

The next day, while performing her daily chores, the shepherd's wife discovered her husband's flute and a divine figurine in her water pot after collecting water from a well. News of this supernatural occurrence spread rapidly throughout the village. Villagers gathered to view the figurine and began worshipping the new idol. Due to its discovery in the mouth of the Shikdi tributary, the idol was named "Shikdu" Devta.

The shepherd returned home safely days later. As time passed, the couple began hearing mysterious noises and whistles in their house. Through a village elder's mediation, the deity requested to be housed in a temple rather than a private residence. Since then, the deity has presided over Rohru. Every April, a grand procession and festivities are held in celebration.

Source: Folk Song.

Dhoban

As a child, I often joined my grandmother and other women from our village on their trips to fetch water. We would carry empty containers and woven baskets as we made our way to the well. The afternoons were protracted and sweltered, with dust from unpaved roads accumulating on our feet; however, the women appeared unperturbed. With each step, their voices gradually increased in volume, initially soft but progressively amplified as more individuals joined. Their song would permeate the air, reminiscent of a melody I had known since time immemorial, lingering like an intergenerational secret, and notably, it possessed a captivating quality—

"काला घगरा सिसयाई के, ओ धोबण पाणीये जो चाँली है म तेरी सो..."

The words intrigued me even before I comprehended their significance. It was a narrative of love, betrayal, and premature death. My grandmother was well versed in the story—she would hum the melody as she filled her vessel, subsequently recounting the tale during our return journey. Her narration imbued the story with a sense of reality, as if the washerwoman still traversed among us, and as if the river continued to whisper her name.

My grandmother called her Chandni. She was a poor laundress, but beautiful nonetheless. Her home was a small hut on the village outskirts, where the river flowed like a shimmering band through the valley. Every evening, she would walk without shoes to fetch water, her dark skirt (locally known as Ghaghara) swaying with each movement, stained deeply with permanent dye. Villagers warned against going too far or staying near the stone stairway leading to the palace grounds. Chandni, however, ignored their cautions—why would a ruler be concerned with a destitute washerwoman?

One night as she prepared to fill her container, she heard a rustling sound behind her. Turning around, she was startled to find a man standing nearby. There was a tall gentleman who was dressed in shimmering silk clothes that caught the dimming light. His eyes were dark and held an unfamiliar, potentially dangerous glint.

"Who are you?" she inquired.

With a mischievous expression, the man scooped up a glossy pebble and hurled it toward her. The small stone produced a faint thud as it landed in close proximity to her feet.

Chandni's expression turned quizzical, her eyebrows knitting together. "I asked—"

"You are beautiful," he interjected. "More beautiful than any woman I have encountered." Anxiety gripped her as she abruptly realized that she was all alone. "I must depart."

While attempting to make her exit up the staircase, she felt his hand suddenly clasp her wrist. Paralyzed with uncertainty, she found herself at a loss for her next move.

"Unhand me," she commanded, striving to control the tremor in her voice as her heart pounded. "I'm nothing more than a woman who washes clothes."

The man advanced and tightened his grip. "What relevance does that hold for me?" Chandni swiftly disengaged herself and ascended the staircase, her pulse quickening. She resisted the urge to glance behind her. Nevertheless, when she returned for water the subsequent evening, he was there. And again, the following night. The prince reached a conclusion: he longed for her.

The arrival of the royal guards at her unpretentious home stirred the village into a flurry of hushed conversations. Without uttering a word, they guided her to the palace, where she was clothed in silken fabrics and adorned with golden accessories that cast a luminous glow on her skin. However, not all palace dwellers were pleased with their presence. The queen, her expression stern and analytical, observed quietly from behind her chamber's elaborate drapery as the washerwoman passed by, unaware of the impending threat lurking in the darkness.

As weeks elapsed, Chandni remained a stranger in the palace, despite her luxurious attire. This fact was evident to both her and the queen. On a particular evening, as the corridors were illuminated by lamps, the queen requested her attendance.

"Join me, cherished sister," she invited, her voice honeyed. Chandni wavered before acquiescing. A tray laden with golden delicacies was presented to the attendees. The queen chose one and positioned it at Chandni's lips.

"Partake," she directed.

Chandni lifted her hand. An aspect of the queen's demeanour unsettled her, yet refusal would breed mistrust. She sampled a portion. The flavour was unusual— saccharine, with an undercurrent of acrimony. She ingested it. The female denizens of the palace observed in silence.

Chandni consumed the second confection. During this time, the individual inhaled abruptly. Her sight grew hazy and her fingers shook. She attempted to rise; however, her limbs felt leaden. The monarch merely observed as Chandni crumpled to the floor. The final sound she detected was laughter before slipping into unconsciousness.

That evening, the current transported her away. She was clothed in matrimonial crimson and positioned on a wooden raft, which was subsequently pushed into the stream. The palace gates remained shut and the prince was secluded in anguish. However, the washerman lingered in the village. He did not encounter his wife for numerous days.

When the raft drifted past him, he relinquished the garments in his hand. He hastened to the water's edge and called her name, but she did not regain consciousness. The river had no response.

My grandmother shook her head, exhaled audibly, and stated, "Her physical attractiveness was both her advantage and her detriment." After which she patted my head and instructed us to retrieve the water before sunset.

Responding to her command, the group of women made their way to the well, maintaining the tune they had been humming throughout their journey.

Source: A regional folk melody, vocalized by the female residents of my village and explained by my maternal grandmother.

The Legend of the River and the Rose

In the agricultural region of Punjab, characterized by expansive fields of golden mustard and gently flowing rivers, resided a young woman named Mehar. Renowned in her village for her aesthetic appeal and benevolence, Mehar's most distinctive trait was her profound affinity for the natural environment, particularly the river that traversed the local terrain. The Sutlej River, as it was designated, served as more than a mere watercourse; it represented a vital resource for the community. Local inhabitants depended on this waterway for crop irrigation, piscatorial pursuits, and potable water procurement. Mehar frequently allocated her afternoon hours to the riverside, where she would intone traditional melodies. Her vocal performances resonated throughout the surrounding valleys, creating a harmonious blend with the ambient sounds of the flowing watercourse.

As Meher sang beside the nearly desiccated riverbed, she spotted an exquisite rose bush in full bloom. The flowers were extraordinary, with petals that gleamed in hues of scarlet and amber. Fascinated, she drew closer to the bush and delicately caressed its petals. To her astonishment, the plant responded in a gentle, musical tone.

The rose bush addressed Meher, saying, "I've been anticipating an individual with a pure spirit to activate my mystical powers. If you pledge to nurture me, I'll grant you a single wish."

Astonished yet eager, Meher contemplated briefly. She had always aspired to bring delight to her village, which had been grappling with a drought for several months. The terrain was parched, and the villagers were facing hardships. With a heart brimming with optimism, she articulated her wish.

"I wish for the river to surge abundantly once more, reinvigorating our fields and restoring happiness to our community," she announced.

The rose bush radiated brilliance, and in a moment, a delicate zephyr swept across the landscape. The Sutlej began to expand, its waters surging with renewed energy. Villagers observed in amazement as the river metamorphosed before their eyes, instilling their hearts with delight and thankfulness.

As the river flowed, the fields blossomed as if by enchantment. Mustard blooms swayed in the breeze, and the villagers celebrated the resurgence of prosperity. Meher emerged as an emblem of aspiration and affection in the village, her connection with the river intensifying.

Yet, as time progressed, Meher discerned the rose bush's deterioration. Its petals lost their brilliance, and the once-vibrant hues faded. Distressed, she hastened to the shrub and inquired, "What ails you, cherished rose?"

The rose bush explained, "My enchantment is linked to the river's current. Your wish has brought happiness to your community, but it has depleted my life force. I require your assistance to regain my power."

Committed to preserving the rose bush, Meher consulted the village's wise elders. They convened beneath the old banyan tree, exchanging stories and insights passed down through time. After extensive talks, they resolved to organize a celebration honoring both the river and rose bush, welcoming all to join.

The villagers collaborated to create traditional meals, design vibrant ornaments, and perform folk melodies that praised their bond with nature. When the festival day arrived, the river glistened in the sunlight, and the atmosphere was filled with cheer and merriment.

As the celebration commenced, Meher stood near the rose bush, her heart brimming with affection for her village and the wonders of the natural world. She guided the villagers in a song that resonated through the fields, a tune that expressed gratitude and solidarity.

"Flow, oh river, flow with grace,

bring life to our fields, our sacred places. With every drop, we honor you,

and the rose that blooms, so pure and true."

The villagers' singing triggered an extraordinary phenomenon. In response to their affection and gratitude, the river's flow intensified. Concurrently, the rose bush began to regain its vigor, its petals growing more vivid with each musical note. The festivities extended into the late hours, with dancing and storytelling surrounding the bonfire. Meher perceived an intricate connection between the river and the rose bush, recognizing their interlinked destinies. The villagers' collective love and harmony rekindled the rose's magical properties, which in turn invigorated the river's current.

Bathed in the moon's silvery radiance that illuminated the terrain, Meher pledged to the rose bush, "You represent the core of our village, and I shall forever value and defend you."

Henceforth, Meher took on the role of steward for the river and rose bush. She educated the villagers about environmental reverence, appreciating its blessings, and coexisting harmoniously with their environment. The river sustained its plentiful flow, and the fields thrived, ushering prosperity into the village.

As time went by, Meher evolved into a respected figure, renowned for her compassion and affinity for the natural world. The rose bush thrived, becoming a representation of endurance and optimism. Villagers frequently congregated near the river's edge, exchanging tales and melodies, and perpetuating the story of Meher and the mystical qualities of the river and rose.

With the passing of seasons, the village remained lively and enduring. The Sutlej River continued its steady flow, sustaining both the land and the spirits of its inhabitants. Whenever the villagers performed their traditional songs, the river appeared to sway, mirroring their elation and appreciation.

Source: Narrated by the villagers of the area.

The Curse of the Natvani

Nestled in the northern part of India, Himachal Pradesh stands as a mountainous jewel, captivating visitors with its enigmatic charm. This state is a realm where age-old legends and folklore continue to thrive within the collective consciousness of its people. Himachal Pradesh boasts an array of natural splendors, a deep-rooted cultural legacy, and thriving spiritual customs. The region is also a repository of intriguing narratives and myths that mirror the historical background, convictions, and ideals of its inhabitants. I'm recounting a story from Sirmour that took place during Raja Madan Singh's rule. This folklore tells of a woman skilled in the dark art of necromancy who presented herself to the Raja to demonstrate her acrobatic prowess.

The origins of Sirmaur District's name are subject to multiple interpretations. One theory suggests it was named "Sirmaur" to reflect its preeminence among hill states, symbolizing its status as the pinnacle or "crown" of all districts. Another explanation traces the name to Sirmour, Raja Rasalu's son and King Shalivahan II's grandson, implying the district adopted his appellation. Sirmaur's religious landscape features local deities like Shirgul Devta at Churdhar, as well as Hindu gods such as Lord Shiva and Parshuram, an avatar of Lord Vishnu at Renuka. The district's most significant event, the Renuka fair, occurs each November near the picturesque lake, attracting large crowds.

In Sirmaur, the predominant linguistic form is Sirmauri, a Hindi dialect. The region is notable for its vibrant cultural traditions, exemplified by the enthusiastic celebration of festivals like Lohri, Baisakhi, and Diwali. A significant aspect of the local cultural identity is the prevalence of traditional artistic forms, including various types of music, dance performances, and handmade crafts.

Agricultural productivity in the Sirmauri Tal region is severely impacted by widespread beliefs in a curse attributed to Natvani, a female entertainer. As a result, many fields remain uncultivated. The local population grapples with persistent challenges, including crop failures, which are further compounded by recurrent landslides and inadequate regional development.

A narrative from the early era of Sirmaur state, under King Madan Singh's reign, is preserved in local lore. The story tells of a female acrobat who exhibited her prowess before the king. Impressed, the monarch proposed a daring challenge: if she could successfully navigate across the Giri River on a rope stretched between Poka Village and Toka Hill, he would reward her with half of his kingdom.

Near Toka Hill, as an acrobat was about to complete her daring performance, Diwan Jujhar Singh, the chief minister, took drastic action. Fearing the loss of half the kingdom, he severed the rope, causing the acrobat to plummet into the Giri River. Legend has it that the fallen performer then placed a curse on the local population, stating: "Ar Toka Par Poka, Doob Maro Sirmoro Re Loka" (translated as: 'With Toka on one side and Poka on the other, may Sirmaur's inhabitants perish by drowning').

The legend recounts that the waterway was subsequently christened the Giri River, and the supposed hex was believed to have unleashed a cataclysmic inundation, effectively erasing the Sirmaur Kingdom from existence.

The oral tradition of this account has been perpetuated through familial lineages, with fathers conveying it to their descendants over multiple generations.

Source: Story narrated by the people of Sirmaur.

The Ghost That Got Away

Situated on the southern escarpment of the Himalaya 'Kangra,' an exquisite district of Himachal Pradesh, there lived 2 friends named Dhania and Kulfi Ram. Being good friends, they would help one another during difficult times. Dhania owned a small grocery shop, whereas Kulfi Ram was a barber and both had been recently introduced to the bliss of marital life, each having brough home a beautiful wife.

One day when Kulfi Ram was busy cutting a customer's hair, Dhania came in haste to meet him. Dhania was more anxious than ever before. At the sight of his pale face Kulfi Ram laughed and asked whether some calamity had fallen on him. Dhania replied in a quavering voice telling his friend about how he is dreading his upcoming visit to his in- laws' place. Dhania never felt comfortable with any form of social interaction. Having heard this Kulfi Ram laughed again questioning his concern and reassuring him that he should be happy with it. Trying to cheer his friend up, he further told him how special her would feel when his in-laws would run around him to look after all his needs.

Dhania now more furious told him about his discomfort and the reasons for his anxiety. The uncertainty of his actions leads him to question his self, further building insecurity. Kulfi Ram now comprehended his friend's troubled state of mind and decided to help him. He reassured him that there was nothing to worry at all and told him about his own experience of visiting his in-law's place after marriage. All his attempts to calm his friend were in vain. Kulfi Ram then decided to accompany him and suggested two things: not to talk unnecessarily and to avoid eating much. Dhania also agreed with these suggestions.

The next day, the two men set out, and in a few hours, they arrived at their destination. The entire family welcomed them. Dhania's mother-in-law greeted them using with folded hands. Dhania did not utter a word and managed to convey his thoughts through facial expressions and by nodding his head slowly. Instead, Kulfi Ram claimed that Dhania was just tired and required sound sleep. Soon after, they were led into the kitchen for dinner. Starving after the long walk, Dhania ate two puris in one go when suddenly Kulfi Ram's words echoed in is mind. While Kulfi Ram sat there eating away steadily, Dhania did not dare pick up another puri.

After the meal, both found themselves in a room with two beds. Dhania woke up in the middle of the night. His stomach making the queerest sounds, rumbling and gurgling. He found himself hungry in the middle of the night. He lay still for some time hoping he would fall asleep but soon realized it was hopeless. He then shook Kulfi Ram to get up and asked him to do something as he was starving. Although irritated, Kulfi Ram rolled out of bed, opened the door, and peeped outside.

On the other side of the courtyard was a room that Kulfi assumed was a store because they had seen Dhania's mother-in-law coming out of that room holding a tin of ghee. The store was certain to eat. Kulfi Ram suggested that they sneak into the store and look around it. To keep an eye out for any member of the household Kulfi Ram decided to stand at a distance from the storeroom and warn Dhania if he saw somebody coming in his direction.

Dhania entered the store through a skylight. At first, he could not see a thing but slowly as his eyes adjusted to the dark, he could make out some shapes- boxes, tins, bottles, buckets, and sacks full of something. After a few minutes, he caught the sight of an earthen pitcher hanging from the roof. He was sure that it contained some edible item. Dhania stood up on a tin box and stretched one arm as far as it would go, however, he could barely reach the pitcher's bottom.

He picked a stick lying nearby and gave the pitcher a smart tap. There was a cracking sound and a thin stream of something began to flow out of the pitcher. Dhania eagerly opened his mouth to catch the stream, took a big gulp, and realized that it was honey. He stood under the pitcher devouring the sweetness.

Lost in gluttony, he did not see the crack at the bottom of the pitcher widen. Suddenly without warning, a large chunk of the pitcher broke away and the thin stream became a torrent. Honey was all over his hair, it got into his eyes and ears and ran down his nose into his kurta. Dripping with honey, all sticky and annoyed, he tried to come down from the tin box on which he stood. The moment he tried to step down, his feet were unable to stay put amidst all the glistening sweet liquid and he fell down on a sack full of wool.

The honey acted like gum and out of the heap rose a ghostly figure. All this happened while Kulfi Ram had no idea since he was had fallen asleep as soon as his friend slipped into the storeroom. He was snoring, lost deep in sleep. Dhania suffocated by the wool and the sticky liquid struggled to free himself and in haste pushed and dropped some tins. The noise woke up Dhania's in-laws as well as Kulfi Ram. As they came running to inspect the source of all the commotion, the door of the storeroom emerged a giant ghastly figure. Upon looking at this demonic silhouette some members of the household fainted and others ran away screaming.

Unlike the others, Kulfi Ram knew that his friend had messed up. He quickly conjured a plan and asked Dhania's father-in-law not to enter storeroom. He told them that he had a knack for dealing with ghosts and spirits promising to do away with this evil spirit. Dhania's father-in-law begged him to do so as soon as possible and locked himself along with the other family members in his own room.

Kulfi Ram strictly ordered everyone to stay quiet and close their eyes and chant a mantra while he went outside to deal with the spirit. Kulfi Ram locked the door of the room from the outside and while chanting mantras ran towards the storeroom where Dhaniya was hiding. He then took Dhania to the well behind the house where

Dhania had a bath and Kulfi buried his sticky clothes in a nearby field. The next morning, they were both greatly admired for their bravery. The two friends returned home, laughing all the way.

Source: Local people of Kangra narrated the story.

The Tragic Tale of Thakur Moni

The Kinnaur Valley, characterized by its imposing mountain ranges and verdant landscapes, serves as the setting for a compelling narrative preserved through generations in the form of a renowned folk song. This cultural artifact, derived from a prominent Kinnauri musical tradition, elucidates the life of Thakur Moni, a young woman whose experiences exemplify the intricate interplay between personal aspirations and societal expectations. The narrative unfolds within a cultural milieu steeped in tradition, exploring the themes of romantic attachment, personal loss, and the profound impact of social norms on the trajectories of female community members. This folk song encapsulates the essence of the Kinnauri culture, offering valuable insights into the complex dynamics that shape individual destinies within this unique societal context.

In Kamru village, Thakur Moni, a member of the prosperous Dudhyan clan, was renowned for her exceptional beauty and vivacious nature. Her heart was captivated by Ganga Sukh, an honorable young man from the Sangla Village Raipaltu clan. Ganga Sukh's family held a distinguished position in Kinnaur society, their reputation built on their substantial holdings of sheep and goats— animals that represented economic prosperity in that era. Both Thakur Moni and Ganga Sukh hailed from families with considerable influence and esteem within their respective communities.

In the picturesque region of Kinnaur, their affection flourished amidst nature's grandeur, where towering peaks seemed to harbor romantic secrets and flowing streams echoed by yearning melodies. However, the prevailing social conventions of the era cast a pall on their connections. In a society where upholding family prestige often trumped individual fulfillment, Thakur Moni's aspirations were dashed when her parents orchestrated her betrothal to Bhagwan Das, an offspring of the Sangchyan lineage from Rogi Village.

Thakur Moni's narrative extends beyond a simple tale of unreciprocated affection; it exemplifies the challenges encountered by numerous young women in Kinnaur. The custom of arranging marriages for daughters without their input was common, and the opinions of girls, like Moni, were frequently disregarded due to the burden of cultural norms. As she unwillingly prepared for her wedding to Bhagwan Das, she wrestled with emotions of disloyalty and hopelessness, cognizant that her affections lay with someone else.

As her wedding day approached, Thakur Moni gathered 17 female companions who were also grappling with the tension between love and duty. Their discussions revealed that Moni's distress was particularly acute. She voiced her frustration, highlighting the disparity between her dreams and reality. "My parents have done me a great disservice," she lamented, "by arranging my marriage to someone I don't love romantically."

Over time, Thakur Moni's unhappiness intensified. Her unfulfilled desires began to take a toll on her mental well-being. Contemplating her situation once more, Thakur Moni bemoans, "I had dreamed of marrying my sweetheart and living in the Raipaltu family's three-story house in Sangla village. However, my parents have wronged me by not allowing me to marry the man I loved and live where I wanted. I've been severely mistreated."

Sadly, Thakur Moni's life ends at the hands of her husband. Suspicion and misunderstanding led to her untimely death. This tragic event irreversibly changed the course of her existence.

The tragic fate of Thakur Moni, who perished in the hands of her husband during a moment of desperation marked by mistrust and failed communication, serves as a poignant illustration of the dire outcomes in a society that often places traditional values above individual well-being. The folk melody recounting her story not only expresses sorrow for her unrealized aspirations, but also functions as a cautionary narrative for subsequent generations, highlighting the potential consequences of such societal priorities.

The discourse surrounding matrimony and female autonomy in Kinnaur has experienced a notable shift in recent years. As societal norms evolve, women's roles and rights undergo significant changes. Education has emerged as a transformative force, enabling young women to pursue aspirations and exercise agencies in selecting their life partners. Contemporary Kinnauri daughters are no longer constrained to being mere elements in familial alliances; instead, they can forge their own paths guided by personal ambitions and inclinations.

Thakur Moni's tragic story has become a powerful force in introspection and societal transformation. Her experiences strike a chord with numerous individuals who have endured comparable hardships, emphasizing the need for empathy and an understanding of personal connections. While we commemorate her life through traditional music and oral narratives, we also acknowledge the advancements made and recognize the challenges that remain to be addressed.

Thakur Moni's story serves as a compelling illustration of love's intricacies, traditional constraints, and the transformative impact of education and personal agency. The evocative melodies of Kinnauri folk songs echo the experiences of women throughout history, whose voices merit recognition, appreciation and respect. By commemorating their narratives, we create a path toward a future where love is not bound by custom, but embraced as a freely made, joyful decision. We must carry forward the insights gained from Thakur Moni's experience, using her tragic circumstances to inspire change and empower future generations to shape their destinies.

Source: Folk Song.

The Legend of the Ban Jhakri

The Kullu Valley's sylvan landscapes have long been associated with an air of enigma. Lofty conifers and deciduous trees stand as motionless guardians, their expansive foliage impeding the penetration of solar illumination. The indigenous populace maintained a conviction that the woodland possessed an ethereal essence, with its safeguarding entrusted to an primordial entity referred to as Ban Jhakri, the custodial spirit.

Legends of its fury and compassion have been transmitted across generations, yet to the youthful and audacious woodsman Shyam, these were merely fables designed to instill fear in youngsters. "Phantoms, entities, guardians! You folks tremble at mere illusions," Shyam derided whenever the village elders cautioned him. On a brisk evening, as his fellow villagers congregated around the communal blaze, they exchanged apprehensive glances. "Shyam," one of the senior residents intoned gravely, "The woodland differs from your agricultural plots or the marketplace. It possesses a life force, and Ban Jhakri stands sentinel over it. Those who fail to show reverence never emerge." Shyam sneered and made a dismissive motion. "I've encountered this warning before, yet I stand here unscathed. I've harvested timber and returned home without fail." "However, you've never traversed the depths of the forest, beyond the consecrated glade," another elder murmured, "That region of the woodland is prohibited."

Undeterred by prohibitions, Shyam was intent on disproving the prevalent tales. Frustrated with the long hours spent felling small trees near the forest's edge while grappling with superstitious fears, he saw an opportunity for financial gain. With winter on the horizon and firewood in high demand, Shyam reasoned that harvesting more timber, especially from the larger trees in sacred areas, could provide him with substantial earnings for an extended period. As dawn broke, Shyam shouldered his axe and set out for the woods with unwavering resolve. Village youth pursued him, pleading for reconsideration. "Shyam bhaiya, turn back!" a young voice cried out. "The Ban Jhakri will seize you!" Shyam quipped, "If I come across this Ban Jhakri, I'll ask him to assist me with the wood!" His mirth vanished as he stepped into the forest's depths.

The familiar chirping of birds and rustling of leaves initially provided solace. As Shyam delved deeper into the forest, however, the temperature plummeted. The once-cheerful light filtering through the foliage dimmed, giving way to a dense, greenish haze. He halted, gripping his axe firmly, recognizing he had entered the hallowed grove where tree-felling was forbidden. The trees here were primordial, their trunks impossibly broad and their limbs laden with moss. The atmosphere was permeated with the aroma of damp soil and decomposing vegetation.

Despite a sense of unease creeping along his spine, Shyam spotted an enormous oak, aware of its timber's high market value. He smirked and tightened his hold on the axe. As he prepared to strike, a sudden gust swept through the grove. The overhead branches groaned, and the leaves seemed to whisper to life.

Shyam faltered, but his pride prevented retreat. "Merely the wind," he murmured, swinging the axe. The blade connected with the oak's trunk, producing a dull thud and splitting the bark. Before he could attempt another blow, a low, guttural voice reverberated through the grove: "Who dares violate my forest?" Shyam pivoted, his heart pounding. The voice was unlike any he had encountered - deep, resonant, and imbued with ancient, primal fury. "Who's there?" he called out, his voice quavering. "Reveal yourself!"

"I implore you! It won't happen again!" He sobbed, tears streaming down his face.

The Ban Jhakri's visage exhibits a blend of grief and wrath. "It's too late now. Your equilibrium is shattered. You will now become an eternal part of the woodland."

As roots enveloped Shyam, his flesh began to petrify. His upper limbs extended into branches, his lower extremities anchored in the earth, and his cries faded into the air. Within moments, he transformed from man to a contorted tree, standing immobile among its fellows. The Ban Jhakri retreated into the darkness, leaving the sacred area in hushed stillness once more.

In the village, people anticipated Shyam's return, but he never materialized. Eventually, some men journeyed into the forest to seek him out. Upon reaching the hallowed grove, they discovered his axe abandoned beside an unfamiliar tree, its twisted limbs reaching skyward as if in torment. The villagers grasped the situation and departed, pledging never to re-enter the sacred space. To this day, Kullu Valley residents warn travelers against venturing too deep into the forest. They claim the Ban Jhakri continues to observe, protect the trees, and penalize those who disturb the serenity.

If you listen intently in the forest's depths, you might catch the whispers of the trees—perhaps Shyam's voice, cautioning others to revere the woodland he once challenged.

Sources

1. *Reference: "Folktales of Himachal Pradesh" by Ramesh Chander Dogra.*

2. *Additional references to Ban Jhakri and related folklore can be found in studies by the Indian Anthropological Society and publications of the Indira Gandhi National Centre for the arts.*

Hadi Rani

Rajasthan's terrain is a testament to extraordinary courage, self-sacrifice, and the practice of jauhar, with each parcel of land echoing tales of heroism. One such narrative from this rich tapestry of history involves a queen of the Chauhan Dynasty from the Hadauti region. This account illustrates a quintessential Rajasthani legend, where a queen's ultimate sacrifice became the catalyst for her husband's participation in combat.

The legendary fortresses of Kota-Bundi serve as enduring monuments to Hadi Rani's honor and courage, with every brick recounting her remarkable story. Hadi Rani, wedded to Rawat Ratan Singh, a Chundawat monarch in Mewar, played a pivotal role in a tumultuous period. When Maharaja Raj Singh summoned Ratan Singh to join the insurrection against the Mughal governor Aurangzeb, the newly married ruler found himself torn. On his wedding night, Rawat Ratan Singh, unaware of the brewing conflict, entered the women's quarters of his palace, anticipating a joyous celebration with his bride 'Haadji', the daughter of Rao Shatrusal of Bundi. However, his plans were suddenly disrupted by the resounding blast of a trumpet, heralding an immediate call to arms.

In the hallway, the melodious strains of the Mangal Geet, sung by women and accompanied by the dulcet tones of the Shehnai, created an ambiance of bittersweet emotion. As Rawat Ratan Singh Chundawat bowed to pay homage to his newlywed bride, the palace resounded with the reverberating call of conch shells, heralding the onset of war. A jolt of excitement coursed through Rawat Ratan Singh's entire being, momentarily distracting him from embracing his spouse. Being ensnared in the throes of romance and hesitant to relinquish the marital bliss and his wife's devotion Rawat Ratan Singh was reminded by Hadi Rani of his responsibilities. She spurred him towards the battlefield by personally handing him a sword.

The sound of the trumpet indicating war blared again, sending another wave of electricity through every nerve of Chundawat's body. Adorned with his armour on his body and armed with weapons, he descends the stairs of his palace roaring "Har Har Mahadev" and mounted his neighing horse.

Upon catching sight of Hadi Rani watching him from the palace window, Rana Ratan Singh's valor faltered, consumed by the fresh passion for his recently wedded spouse. He instructed his servants to visit Rani's quarters and procure a personal possession from his wife to serve as a token of remembrance.

Hadi Rani understood that her husband was caught in a web of love, which would keep him away from his kshatriya duty. She then decided what memento should be given to her husband as a keepsake, so that he could turn away from the web love and remain steadfast on his kshatriya dharma and duty to fight this upcoming war without any worries.

Hadi Rani did not want to see her husband away from war, so as a last token she decided to cut off her head and sent it to her husband. As she was an obstacle to her husband's duty, she did this so that he could be free from attachment and perform his duty in the battle field like a brave warrior. The servant covered the chopped-off head with cloth and gave it to Ratan Singh. The head was completely soaked in blood, but the kajal applied to the eyes was intact because while the Rani chopped off her head with her own hand, not a single drop of tear was shed from her eyes.

When her head reached Rana Ratan Singh, he wore it like a necklace around his neck and shouted "Har Har Mahadev." It is said that when he wore his wife's head like an armour, he wore it like the embodiment of her own courage and valour and fought fiercely across the battlefield, creating fear and panic amidst the Mughal army.

Rana Ratan Singh emerged as a glorious fighter, a kshatriya who followed his dharma and fulfilled his duty after the brave sacrifice of his wife, that opened his eyes and made him realize his true duty towards his motherland. When the battle, the great rebellion, was over, he got to his knees and cut off his own head, having lost the desire to live, for the pain and agony to live without his wife could not let him live.

Hadi Rani, who on seeing her husband turn away from the battlefield, cut off her head for the sake of her motherland, and dharma of Kshatriyani, is still worshipped in the land of Rajasthan and folk singers through their songs have immortalized this tale of valour.

Although death is an inescapable reality for all, some individuals transcend mortality through their enduring legacy. These remarkable people continue to inspire countless others across generations, their influence persisting long after they have departed from this world.

Source: Folk Songs of Rajasthan.

Whispers of the Lake

Himachal Pradesh, renowned for its picturesque valleys, serene lakes, and sacred temples, is often referred to as Devbhumi due to the numerous shrines dedicated to various deities. Among these divine figures, devta Kamrunag, also known as Badadev, holds a significant position in the region's mythology. According to ancient lore, Kamrunag vowed to his mother that he would perpetually support the vulnerable and fight on their behalf. To assess his prowess Lord Krishna devised a test challenging Kamrunag, who had to pierce all the leaves of a sacred fig tree with a single arrow. In an attempt to complicate the task, Krishna concealed one leaf beneath his foot. Remarkably, Kamrunag's arrow successfully penetrated every leaf, including the hidden one. This extraordinary demonstration of skill caused Krishna to grow apprehensive about the Pandavas' chances of victory. He surmised that if Kamrunag were to align with the Kauravas, they would likely defeat the Pandavas, potentially resulting in the triumph of Adharma over Dharma.

According to lores and mythology, Kamrunag's fervent dedication to Bhagwan Vishnu led Shri Krishna, a Vishnu avatar, to seek his head. Kamrunag joyfully obliged, offering his decapitated head to Vishnu while expressing a desire to observe the entire Mahabharata conflict. To honor this request, Shri Krishna, with the Pandavas' assistance, secured Kamrunag's head to a bamboo tree. Bheema then formed a massive water-filled crater with a single strike to quench dev Kamrunag's thirst. After the Pandavas emerged victorious in the Mahabharata war, they presented Kamrunag with jewelry as a token of appreciation. Additionally, Krishna bestowed upon Kamrunag a blessing, ensuring his veneration during the Kali Yuga and granting him the power to fulfill humanity's wishes.

The Badadev Kamrunag temple and its associated lake are nestled in the Mandi district's mountainous terrain in Himachal Pradesh during the Kaliyuga period. A lush deodar forest envelops the lake. Situated 60 km from Mandi, accessing the temple requires a arduous uphill journey on foot. Renowned as the deity of precipitation, Badadev Kamrunag is believed to bestow rainfall when worshippers approach with steadfast resolve and earnest prayers.

The waters of Kamrunag Lake are adorned with an abundance of gold and silver ornaments, offerings made by those whose prayers have been answered. Remarkably, this treasure trove remains unguarded, as it is said that Dev Kamrunag himself watches over the valuables. Intriguingly, these precious items are reported to vanish from the lake's depths within a matter of two to three days.

A woman, having given birth to several daughters, yearned for a male child. She vowed to sacrifice her golden earrings in exchange for this blessing. Her unwavering devotion to Bada dev Kamrunag impressed the deity, who subsequently granted her wish. Upon the birth of her son, she journeyed to the Kamrunag Temple to fulfill her promise.

As she prepared to cast her ornaments into the sacred lake, doubt crept into her mind. She began to consider that perhaps it was merely her destiny to bear a son after five daughters, rather than divine intervention. Despite her wavering faith, she ultimately followed through with her pledge. Upon arriving home with her infant son, the woman experienced thirst and decided to rest. She discovered a stream nearby and approached it to quench her thirst. As she cupped her hands to drink, her earrings suddenly reappeared, and her child passed away immediately afterward. It is said that Badadev restored her jewelry as punishment for her impure thoughts and lack of gratitude for divine blessings. Since that day, it is believed that those who sincerely pray to God will have their wishes fulfilled.

The Almighty blesses humanity generously, yet He rejects any form of deceit or misconduct.

Source: My mom passed down this regional story to me.

The Eternal Gurdians of the Western Himalayas

Mahasu Devta, revered as the supreme ruler of mortals and gods, is one of four divine brothers—Botha, Chalda, Bashik, and Pabasi—collectively known as Mahasu. These deities, like many others in the Himalayas, are worshipped across villages, with each village often having its own family gods (Kul Devta) or goddesses (Kul Devi).

In the Shimla region of Himachal Pradesh, formerly called the Mahasu District, Mahasu Devta holds sway over dozens of villages. Villagers seek their deities' guidance on health, disputes, and livelihoods through the human mediums. Deities travel within their territories in palanquins and convene during festivals or temple inaugurations, thus extending their influence.

Mahasu's jurisdiction spans parts of Uttarakhand, Shimla and Sirmaur. Subordinate deities, known as birs, serve as soldiers or ministers, with some, such as Sherkulia, gaining independent recognition as devtas. The administration of Mahasu temples includes roles such as wazir (head), priests, assistants, and equipment keepers, traditionally passed down within Brahmin and Rajput families. This tale explores the origins of Mahasu Devta and their heroic intervention in the Himalayas.

According to the legend, the Mahasu brothers migrated from Kashmir to liberate the region from a demon, Kirmir, who terrorized the people.

Kirmir resided in a pond near Mendrath, demanding sacrifices of rice, goats, and even villagers. A Brahmin, Huna Bhat, lost five of his six sons to the demon. When his wife, Kalavati, went to fetch water, Kirmir attacked her, vowing to have her for himself soon. As she ran for her life, she heard a celestial voice.

The voice belonged to Shedkulia bir, a minister who accompanied the Mahasu brothers. He assured Kalavati of the demon's impending defeat and vowed to protect her remaining son. Shedkulia, who resided far away from the village of Mendrath asked Kalavati what reward she would offer if he saved her last son. She promised that he would rule land and people would worship him. Shedkulia revealed that he and three other ministers served as Mahasu bodyguards in a pond in Kashmir. Together with the Mahasu brothers, they could defeat the demon, but Kalavati's husband, Huna Bhat, needed to summon them.

Kalavati agreed and hurried home, but by the time she arrived, she had transformed into stone and could no longer speak. The villagers and her husband, Huna Bhat, used rituals to bring her back to her senses. She recounted her encounter and urged Huna Bhat to journey to Kashmir to call Mahasu.

Though the villagers encouraged him, Huna Bhat was filled with doubt, fearing a perilous journey through rugged terrain and dense forests, as no one had ever returned from such a mission before. The villagers were disheartened by Huna Bhat's reluctance. However, his wife reminded him of their immense loss and despair and urged him to act. Moved by her words and love for their son, Huna Bhat resolved to undertake a dangerous journey to save his child.

Before departing on this mission, Huna Bhat went to Hatkoti, where he had previously heard of an elderly Brahmin, Pundiyan who knew a secret route to Kashmir. On arrival, Huna Bhat found that Pundiyan was blind and old. Refusing food until granted an audience, Huna Bhat finally met the Brahmin, touched his feet and sought his guidance. Pundiyan promised to help, urging Huna Bhat to eat and prepare for their discussion.

After their meal, the blind Pundiyan cautioned Huna Bhat about the perilous journey to Kashmir, describing treacherous mountains, rivers, dense forests, wild animals, and strange obstacles like dancing villagers and icy snowdrifts. Despite these warnings, Huna Bhat remained resolute, driven by his love for his son.

Moved by his determination, Pundiyan provided detailed direction and advice asking his devi Hateshwari for her aid. The next morning, the Huna Bhaat was set off. Along the way, he encountered all the challenges Pundiyan described but, with the blessings of Hateshwari, overcame them with ease, eventually reaching Kashmir safely. After days of travel, Huna Bhat reached the pond where Mahasu and the birs resided. Shedkulia bir, the voice Kalavati had heard, awaited him. Shedkulia hid Huna Bhaat in the temple of Angaru

Devta and warned him to stay hidden, as the other birs might come searching for him.

Shedkulia convinced the devtas to emerge from the pond where they had been living as snakes. Chalda Mahasu, sensing Huna Bhaat's presence, refused to go outside to avoid harming the Brahmin. The birs— Kapala, Kaulu, and Kyala— searched for the Brahmin but, under Shedkulia's influence, overlooked the temple where Huna Bhat was hidden. Meanwhile, Chalda Mahasu stayed firm in his resolve.

The devta sent Shedkulia bir to search for the Brahmin. Shedkulia returned to the temple where Huna Bhaat was hiding and instructed him to carry the palanquin of Chalda Mahasu, who would turn left, while the other gods would turn right. He reassured Huna Bhat and advised him to avoid fearing any noise.

Shedkulia reported back to the devtas claiming that no one was hiding. Trusting him the devtas emerged from the pond in their palanquins. Following Shedkulia's advice, Huna Bhat identified Chalda Mahasu's palanquin and stepped out with it. Voices cried for him to stop but he did not.

The devtas convened a meeting by placing the Huna Bhaat at the center. Bashik Devta asked, "Where are you from, and why have you come here?" Huna Bhaat then addressed the devtas: "O devtas, I am a Brahmin from Kiran Desh. On my land, there are no gods or rulers to protect us. The demon Kirmir terrorizes us. Our king made a treaty with him to lessen his terror, but we still suffer. Every seventh Sunday, we must offer cooked rice, a goat, and every month, a man. Many perished, including five of my six sons. I beg you to come to my land and rid us of this demon."

Bashik Devta asked, "What will you offer us if we come?" Huna Bhat replied, "You will inherit my land and rule over it. Beyond it, many kingdoms await your conquest."

The gods agreed and Chalda Mahasu gave Huna Bhaat a garland, instructing him:

"Take this garland and immerse it in the pond of Maindrath. Perform a havan-yagna for seven days with seven bachelor's boys and seven calves, all while fasting. On the seventh day, plough the field using a new untouched golden plough and silver rope. We will come then."

Huna Bhaat returned home, immersed the garland in the village pond, and gathered seven boys to prepare for the ritual as instructed. Huna Bhaat fasted and performed havans with seven calves. Exhausted by the sixth day and ridiculed by the people, he prematurely plowed the field using a silver rope and a golden plow. This act caused misfortune, and while the Mahasu brothers Bashik, Botha, Pavasi, and Chalda emerged from the land, each bore injuries from the ploughshare and sat in the laps of their birs along with an army of their own.

The devtas appeared first eliminating the exploitative merchant Natola, who had sacrificed the poor to the demon Kirmir. The Mahasus then sough the demon so Huna Bhaat led them to the pond. Kaulu struck the demon in the water, forcing him to flee. As he escaped, other warriors attacked him. The demon fled to Katai Jaan (Kuddu), where the Mahasus caught him. Cornered, Kirmir pleaded for mercy with folded hands but did not heed Kirmir's plea for mercy and killed him. His flesh was consumed by the warriors, and he became known as god Jivaslu. After defeating Kirmir, the Mahasus and their warriors conquered Arakot Casta by dividing it into three parts. They then traveled to Raithik, where they defeated Queen Hurendi and her kingdom. Mahasu Devta later conquered Raigi, defeating King Shigudiya Swagal, and taking his golden horn.

At a meeting in Chauridhar, Mahasus divided territories. Botha Mahasu requested that he Maindrath be granted. Bashik Devta asked for Hanol, and Botha Mahasu, despite being handicapped, insisted on it. After some discussion, Bashik agreed to give Hanol to Botha Mahasu with a condition, which sparked curiosity among the others. Bashik Devta agreed to Botha Mahasu's request for Hanol on the condition that he would be Bashik's guest for a year. Similar arrangements were made for the other deities, including Pavasi Mahasu and Chalda Mahasu. Chalda Mahasu, initially angry, accepted the offer as Bashik's guest for twelve years, and later, Botha Mahasu invited him to stay for a night after twelve years. The gods settled in various places, including Hanol, Akharet, and Devti Dev Forest, where they began their worship.

The Jagra festival, a major event for Mahasu's followers, is a time when people return home to their villages. It is a religious holiday and reunion for families. Observing Jagra is essential for followers, with at least one person from each family attending. The Jagra festival, derived from "jagran" meaning staying awake all night, celebrates the arrival of the Mahasu brothers from Kashmir to Maindrath. It typically falls in Bhadra (August–September), often on the fourth day, coinciding with the Ganesh Chaturthi. In some places, they are celebrated the next day, allowing people to attend both events.

The day before Jagra, temple management members quickly, including pujari, thani, and bhandari. On Jagra days, prasads, including puri, halva, rice, and dal, were prepared. In the morning, the villagers perform purification rituals at holy water sources. The temple courtyard was set up with a burning pole (chira) and a sign (nishan) of Botha. Pujari and religious figures perform rituals, while music is played by bajgis, and villagers receive blessings from Mahasu. The Raja of Jubbal traditionally participates in Jagra, although his son now represents the royal family. Upon arrival, the men light torches and walks in circles, singing the birsu, a song praising Mahasu and his family. This torch-lighting custom is mainly in Himachal Pradesh, with some villages in Bangan and Jaunsar-Bawar following it, whereas others only light the chira. After the puja, the chira is lit from the torches and the prasad is distributed.

Torch lighting is traditionally thought to expel evil spirits, but today, especially among the younger generation, it is seen as a tribute to Mahasu. Similar changes are evident in other local events, such as the Bishu festival, which marks a new year with archery displays in Jaunsar-Bawar. While this custom is less prominent in Himachal Pradesh, it remains strong in some areas, such as Chirgaon. Participation in traditional events is still valued, but modern obligations such as work and education affect local customs. In the Jubbal region, local Pahari traditions linked to temples are declining, while modernized fairs and pan-Hindu festivals are rising, especially in Rampuri and Rohru. These fairs, celebrating deities such as Mahasu and Shikru, include sports, music, and vendors, but are not temple-based. They received state support and became more secular.

Local deities influence sociopolitical matters, and their decisions affect reality. Mahasu brothers' management includes wazirs who oversee different regions. The wazir of the shathi has an advantage in managing the main temple in Hanol, while priests, assistants, and accountants (kardars) independently manage temples. Priests, known as pujaris or deopuzia, perform rituals and life-cycle rites, usually passed down through families.

Bajgis (musicians) play drums and trumpets during Mahasu's puja to appease the deities, promote possession, and provide income. They also participate in life-cycle rites and preserve oral traditions such as Mahasu's katha. All musicians in the Jubbal region are referred to as dhakiss. Mahasu Devta, revered in the Western Himalayas, remains a central figure in the region's cultural and spiritual life. The four deities—Botha, Chalda, Bashik, and Pabasi—hold a vital place across Himachal Pradesh and Uttarakhand. Rituals, administrative systems, and devotion to Mahasu reflect the region's enduring traditions, especially during the Jagra festival, which is a vibrant expression of community, identity, and continuity.

Although some customs, such as the daily lighting of the chira, have declined, core worship practices remain strong. The involvement of the local community, including the Raja of Jubbal and the roles of wazirs and pujaris, shows the adaptability of these traditions to modern times. The fusion of modern elements with local fairs and support from state institutions highlights the balance between tradition and change.

In conclusion, Mahasu Devta's legacy is through his followers, who continue to honor their deities with devotion. The Jagra festival, blending religious rituals with cultural celebrations, ensures that Mahasu's influence remains alive, guiding future generations and preserving the rich heritage of the region.

Source: Ancestral narratives and cultural stories transmitted orally across successive generations within our local community.

Hun Dass Chaukidara

Hun Dass Chaukidara is not merely a tale of moral decay but a reflection on the intricate tapestry of human emotion. This serves as a reminder that our choices, driven by desire and desperation, can reverberate through the lives of many and leave an indelible mark on the course of fate. As it continues to echo the valleys of Himachal Pradesh, this story reminds us to remain vigilant about our own desires and their potential repercussions in the grand narrative of life.

The folktale revolves around the story of a struggling thief who resorted to minor crimes to sustain his family. One day, he conceived a plan for a major heist where he infiltrated the royal palace. Recognizing the heavy security around the treasury, he opted to focus on the king's chambers. Stealthily entering, he observed the sleeping monarch and queen, who appeared to be in a state of semi-consciousness. He patiently waited for her to fall asleep.

Over time, he attempted to verify her state by peering through the curtains. However, his movement caused the vase to slip from his grasp, shattering, and alerting the queen. Before he escaped, she confronted him with a drawn sword: the thief immediately prostrated himself, begging for mercy, and confessing his motives when questioned.

The queen spared his life on one condition that he eagerly accepted without knowing the terms. For his astonishment, she demanded sexual intercourse. Shocked, the thief protested, claiming that he was merely a criminal and not driven by lust. The queen, who was consumed by desire, threatened his life if he refused. Despite his pleas, the patient remained unyielding. In a desperate attempt, the thief requested use of a washroom.

Granted permission, he attempted to flee, but was apprehended by a guard at the exit. After hearing the thief's tale, the guard proposed his own condition for the thief's freedom: return to the queen with an ultimatum - either kill the king or allow the guard to execute the thief before complying with her demands.

Reluctantly, the thief conveys this message to the queen. Blinded by passion, she immediately slayed her sleeping husband. Upon seeing the blood on her clothes and face, she fainted, realizing the gravity of her actions. Her scream alerted the palace, and the news of the king's death spread rapidly. The guard, hearing the commotion, arrived, but feigned ignorance of the situation.

The following day, as funeral preparations commenced, the guilt-stricken queen, adhering to tradition, resolved to immolate herself on the king's funeral pyre. Following tradition, family members and servants approached the funeral pyre in turn, adding wood and paying their respects. Watchman was last to come forward. As he placed wood on the pyre, he inquired, "Queen, please disclose who took the king's life."

Surprised by the inquiry, the queen's eyes opened, and she responded,' There's a cottage in the woods near the kingdom's edge. Seek out an elderly woman She will reveal the king's killer." The pyre bursts into flames and the queen is self-immolated. The mystery of the king's murderer remains unresolved.

Several days later, the watchman journeyed to the location where the queen described and encountered the elderly woman. He then repeated his questions. The old woman guided him outside the cottage and instructed, "Notice the tethered goat? You must decapitate it. Its head becomes airborne. Grasp its ear, and the flying head will guide you to the answer you seek."

The watchman follows these directions. He clutched the ear of an airborne goat head, which led him to a remote area in the forest. This spot was the demon's residence. The demon was absent and his daughter was alone at home. Detecting an outsider's presence, the demon's daughter emerges from her dwelling. She was enchanted by the watchman's appearance and was transformed into a stunning woman. The watchman was enthralled for her beauty and fell under her spell. He forgotten his mission entirely and remained there. At night, the demon's daughter would transform him into various creatures - a parrot, crow, pigeon, or mosquito - and during the day, when the demon was away, she would restore his human form. The watchman enjoyed this peculiar existence for a time but eventually began to long for his home and family. The demon's daughter also grew tired of him. Seizing an opportunity, the watchman escaped and returned home, elating to reunite with his wife and son.

Over time, the watchman began to miss the demon's daughter. Her beautiful vision continues to appear in his mind. He yearned to see her again, and one day quietly left his home and set off for the forest. He attempted to locate the spot but was unsuccessful. Exhausted, he returned to an elderly woman and begged for direction. She replied, "You can find your way back, but it will require another sacrifice."

The watchman asked, "Of whom?" The old woman answered, "Your son."

Driven by desire, the watchman hurried home, took his innocent son, and brought him to an elderly woman.

As he raised his sword to behead his son, the old woman halted him and gently asked, "Hun Dass Chaukidara! Who killed the king?"

As can be seen, the story meanders through treachery, desire, and fateful decisions, and it encapsulates the broader themes prevalent in folk tales—a cautionary narrative reminding us of the thin line that separates the mundane from the mystical. The characters within, particularly the queen and the thief, represent the conflicting aspects of human nature, illustrating how desperation can drive one to surrender to darker impulses, ultimately leading to catastrophic outcomes

Source: Story told by a family member.

The Bride of Churdhar: A Tale of Lost Love

The allure of Himachal Pradesh's deep-rooted history has captivated visitors for generations. Known as the "Land of Gods," this state is distinguished by its mountainous landscape, blanketed in pine forests and snow, and steeped in mythical traditions. Among its numerous enigmatic locations, Churdhar stands out as both the region's highest summit and a silent custodian of ancient tales. Its lush woodlands, swirling mists, and challenging trails have been privy to countless narratives, some openly shared, others shrouded in secrecy. This account aims to uncover one such legend—a tale emerging from Churdhar's depths, where the line between reality and fantasy blurs, and adventurous hikers tread warily alongside the supernatural. This narrative transcends typical ghost stories and curses, revealing how nature harbors mysteries far more ancient and ominous than we can comprehend.

Our expedition delves into the core of Churdhar, where one must heed the faint whispers carried on the breeze and the soft sounds of unseen steps. Looming over Shimla's valleys, Churdhar Peak stands as a mysterious sentinel, veiled in clouds and enigma. This revered mountain is believed to possess sacred qualities, its rocky expanses and wooded areas resonating with the hushed voices of age-old spirits. In the communities nestled at the mountain's base, a spine-chilling narrative circulates—a tale intertwining passion, deceit, and vengeance.

In a distant past, a quaint settlement lay at the foot of Churdhar Mountain. The villagers led uncomplicated lives, attuned to the cycles of their natural surroundings. One resident, a young woman named Mayna, stood out for her captivating vocal abilities. As twilight descended and the sun retreated behind the peaks, Mayna would position herself near the village well, her melodious voice filling the air. Her songs painted vivid pictures of romance, yearning, and the majestic mountains that dominated their landscape. Fellow villagers often suspended their tasks to listen, and it seemed that even the mountain air grew still to catch her harmonious tunes.

One day, a stranger came to the village. His name was Dev. He was a man from the plains, with smooth words and stories of a distant land. He spoke of cities filled with gold, markets bursting with color, and comforts that the villagers had never imagined. Dev was captivated by Mayna, and slowly won her trust and affection. He promised her life beyond the mountains and a life full of joy, wealth, and adventure. Their love blossomed quickly, and soon Dev asked for Mayna's hand in marriage. The village celebrates the union with great joy. The wedding was a grand affair filled with music, dances, and blessings. As per tradition, newlyweds climbed Churdhar the morning after their wedding to seek blessings from the mountain deity. It was believed that those who honored this ritual would be protected and blessed with prosperity. However, Dev was not a man he seemed to have. Beneath his charm and love, he hids a dark secret. He heard ancient tales of treasures hidden within Churdhar gold, jewels, and riches buried deep in the caves. His real reason for marrying Mayna was to use her knowledge of the mountains to find these riches.

The morning after the wedding, Mayna and Dev began to climb Churdhar. The villagers waved them off and were unaware of Dev's greed. As they walked, the thick forest slowly gave way to rocky paths. The air became colder, and heavy silence engulfed them. After hours of climbing, Dev stopped. His eyes, once warm, now burned with desire, "Show me where the treasure is hidden," he demanded. Mayna looked at him as confused and frightened, "What treasure? The mountain is sacred. There are no riches here meant for us." However, the face of Dev is angry. He grabbed her roughly by the arm and screamed, "Don't lie to me! I know the stories. You will take me there, or you will regret it." Tears filled with Mayna eyes. She tried to pull away and pleaded with him to return. The Dev was blinded to his greed and grew violently. At the time of rage, he shoved her hard.

Mayna stumbled, lost her footing, and fell off the cliff. Her scream echoed through the valley before being silenced by rocks below. The patient stood frozen for a moment, and his chest heaved. Coldly, he turned and continued his search for treasure. However, the mountains changed. The wind stopped blowing off. The forest remains unnatural. No bird sang, leaves rustled. Even Dev's footsteps made no sound. The air was heavier and colder. Then, in silence, he heard it—a soft, haunting melody. It was Mayna's voice, singing the songs she once sang well by the village. The sound seemed to have come from everywhere and nowhere. Dev's heart pounded. He spun around, and she was Mayna. Her face was as pale as snow and her eyes were dark and hollow. The bridal clothes were torn and stained with blood and dust. However, her lips moved slowly, singing the same, gentle tune. "You sought riches," her voice echoed though her mouth barely moved, "Now you shall find them." Dev's breath was caught in the throat. He turned and ran and stumbled over the rocks and roots. However, the mountain seemed to twist and turn, leading him into circles. The cliffs loomed closer and the shadows moved where they were not. Mayna's songs grew louder and chased him. He saw figures in the mist faces while watching him and whispers in the wind. The ground crumbled beneath him, and the unseen hands seemed to pull him back. He screamed but the mountain swallowed the sound. When the villagers found him days later, he barely survived. His eyes were wide due to terror, and he muttered endlessly about a singing bride and the mountain's curse. He spoke of shadows and voices that would prevent him from going.

Dev died soon after. His body was untouched, but his mind was shattered beyond repair. The villagers mourned Mayna deeply. However, as time passed, something strange began to occur. During twilight hours, as gusts swept through the pine forest, the ethereal melodies of Mayna's ballads echoed softly. Villagers reported spectral sightings of a figure clad in a ragged wedding gown, perched atop the cliffs, her gaze fixed upon the settlement below. Apprehension gripped the community as they began to believe Mayna's essence had merged with Churdhar, becoming its sacred guardian. Legends circulated that she manifested before those harboring avarice, forewarning them of the mountain's impending wrath. Wayfarers traversing the region occasionally recounted hearing a woman's voice carried on the breeze or glimpsing a spectral form weaving between the trees. Some hastily departed, uttering hushed prayers, while others left offerings of mountain blossoms, confectionery, or modest trinkets at the mountain's base to venerate Mayna and implore her protection.

Source: This narrative was imparted to me by my grandmother.

Rul Kul Devi

A long time ago, in the heart of Himachal Pradesh, which was surrounded by the towering peaks of the Himalayas, a beautiful and ancient kingdom called Vijaypur existed. This kingdom is known for its breathtaking natural beauty, lush green valleys, and crystal-clear rivers. The people of Vijaypur lived in harmony with nature; their fields flourished with golden crops, and their homes were filled with laughter and songs. The land was ruled by a king, who cared deeply for his people and ensured peace and happiness.

However, these events took unexpected turns. A terrible drought struck the kingdom, turning the once-fertile fields into dry parched land. The rivers that once flowed gracefully were on the verge of drying. Silence fell as the crops withered under the scorching sun and no water. People who once had a known abundance were now struggling to find food and water. Despair descended upon once-vibrant land fueled by widespread hunger. The king was devastating. During the day and night, he watched his people suffer, feeling powerless. He sought advice from his council of ministers, but no solution seemed strong enough to break the drought curse. He prayed desperately at the temples, seeking divine guidance, but the skies remained silent. Determined to save his people, the king began fasting, hoping that his sincere prayers would be heard by the gods.

One fateful night, as he lay exhausted from days of worry and fasting, the king dreams, unlike any other. In this dream, he found himself standing in a magical, glowing realm where everything shimmered with a divine light. Before him appeared, Rul Kul Devi, the powerful goddess of the mountains, whose presence filled the air with both awe and serenity. She listened patiently as the king poured out his grief, pleading for her help in saving his kingdom from ruin.

Rul Kul Devi, moved by the king's sincerity and love for his people, offered a solution—but it came with a heavy price. She demanded sacrifice—his son's life. The king was horrified. His son was the future of his dynasty, and the child was raised with love and care. How could he possibly give up his only heir, even to save his kingdom? With a heavy heart, he refused the goddess's demands and was unable to bear the thought of losing his son.

The goddess, unmoved, offered the second choice. At this time, she asked for the sacrifice of a cat, a sacred animal believed to bring about misfortune if harmed. Although it seemed a minor price compared to his son's life, the king hesitated again. He feared eternal punishment in the seven hells to take on the life of an innocent creature. Once again, he declined.

Growing impatient, Rul Kul Devi presented a third option. She asked the king to sacrifice his entire granary, the source of food for his kingdom. Though desperate, the king knew that this choice would only cause further suffering. Without the stored grain, his people would surely starve even more than they had already been. The idea of condemning his subjects to hunger while trying to save them seems cruel. Again, he refused.

Finally, the goddess offered a fourth and final choice: sacrificing his daughter-in- law. The king's heart is then attached. His daughter-in-law was a gentle soul known throughout the Kingdom for her beauty, kindness, and wisdom. She was dearly loved by the people and was at the heart of his family. However, the weight of his suffering bore heavily on his shoulders. Reluctantly, with tears streaming down his face, he agrees. He could not observe his entire kingdom.

The king awoke from the dream, and his heart is heavy with grief. Though it pained him deeply, he knew he had to keep his words to the goddess. He summoned his ministers and revealed the divine command. The news spread quickly throughout the Kingdom, and a dark cloud of sorrow settled over the people. The daughter-in-law, although shocked and heartbroken, accepted her fate with remarkable courage. She understood the importance of the situation and chose to protect the kingdom from her sacrifice.

The day of sacrifice arrived. The entire kingdom gathered at the base of the sacred mountain, where a grand altar was built for the ceremony. The daughter-in-law, dressed in simple ceremonial robes, walked gracefully toward the altar, and her eyes reflected both sadness and strength. The people watched somber silence and their hearts aching for her.

As the final moment approached, brilliant light descended from the sky. The air was filled with divine music and the entire crowd was gasped in awe. Rul Kul Devi herself appeared, radiant and powerful, her face no longer stern but filled with compassion. She raised her hands and stopped the ceremony.

The goddess spoke of her voice echoing the mountains. "King of Vijaypur, you have shown great courage and selflessness. I did not seek blood but to test the depth of your devotion to your people. Your love for your people and your willingness to sacrifice what is dearest to you has moved me."

Turning to the daughter-in-law, she continued, "You are pure of heart, and your sacrifice will not be needed."

In her words, the skies darkened momentarily before heavens burst open with rain. The long-awaited downpour soaked the parched earth, filling the rivers once more, and bringing life back to the land. The crops flourished again, the people rejoiced, and their prayers finally answered.

The king fell to his knees and was overwhelmed by gratitude. From that day forward, he ruled with renewed wisdom, remembering the trials he had faced and the lessons learned. The Kingdom of Vijaypur prospered once more, and the story of Rul Kul Devi's test was passed down through generations, a reminder that true leadership lies in compassion, sacrifice, and unwavering love for one's people.

Sources:https://www.youtube.com/watch?v=DejLUFs2roY Taken from a Himachali song, and dictated by my mother.

Rukmani Kund

An ancient legend from the Bilaspur district of Himachal Pradesh tells of a time when the region was struck by a terrible famine. The scarcity of water caused immense suffering among the people, leaving the king distressed and uncertain about how to proceed.

During a night's slumber, the king experienced a divine visitation from the goddess Rul Kul. He shared his troubles with her and sought her guidance. The goddess proposed several solutions, each requiring a sacrifice. First, she requested the king's son, which he declined to preserve his lineage. Next, she suggested a cat, but the king refused, fearing damnation in the afterlife. When she asked for his house's broom, he again declined, worried about losing his wealth. Finally, the goddess demanded the sacrifice of his daughter-in-law, to which the king readily agreed.

That same evening, the king penned a letter to his daughter-in-law, inviting her home and proposing a pilgrimage to Mata Rul Kul. Upon reading the letter by lamplight, she wept. As she went to fetch water, she encountered a crowing crow and, annoyed, addressed it, mentioning the letter from her father-in-law. Returning home, she requested clothing from her mother for the journey to her in-laws' house. Despite her mother's warning about leaving on an inauspicious Tuesday, she insisted on going, stating she couldn't refuse her father-in-law's request as she might have done for her mother-in-law.

At her in-laws' home, a priest began a ritual while the daughter-in-law stood as a builder encased her in bricks. She instructed the builder to cover her legs and waist, hoping to briefly reunite with her parents in the afterlife. As the bricks reached her shoulders, she asked that her mouth remain uncovered, anticipating a final conversation with her husband.

Water began to flow, signaling the goddess's acceptance of the sacrifice. The tale concludes with a lament about the future of women.

When the story was transmitted by the word of mouth or in its traditional versions as well a question was often asked at the end of the story that is, "Why do you weep, forest dwellers? The village is awash with water."

The answer to which the answer is often simple "The father-in-law may find new daughters-in-law, but parents can never replace their daughter."

Source: Story heard during childhood.

Chaunidhar Shiva Temple

Within the Hindu cosmology, Shiva holds a paramount status as the ultimate divine entity. Hindu theological doctrine ascribes to Shiva the cosmic functions of universal genesis, sustenance, and annihilation. Adherents have established myriad sacred edifices for the veneration of Shiva, extending beyond the Indian subcontinent to various global locations. Nestled in the lush forests of Shimla, atop an elevated landscape, stands a temple devoted to Lord Shiva, boasting a significant historical background. The Chaunridhar Shiva Temple, situated in Haridevi, holds great importance among the area's inhabitants. This revered site is located six kilometers away from Shimla, accessible via the road that links Ghanahati and Kalihatti.

The sacred structure serves as a testament to supernatural occurrences and celestial assistance, with numerous tales passed down through time recounting instances of divine favor and healing. Worshippers frequently share how their heartfelt supplications were fulfilled after a genuine journey to the hallowed grounds, where many report sensing an unexplainable bond with Lord Shiva. These narratives go beyond simple legends, acting as a source of motivation and optimism for the local populace. The prevalent notion that the sanctuary was supernaturally situated at this spot strengthens the view of the temple as a hub of metaphysical power, a concept deeply rooted in the minds of those who visit.

The Chaunridhar Temple's inception is woven into local mythology, merging the extraordinary with the ordinary. The narrative begins with a peculiar event that captured the villagers' attention. A cow, typically known for its gentle nature and predictable habits, started exhibiting unusual behavior that intrigued the local community.

This particular bovine would consistently separate from its herd, journeying to a specific spot on the village periphery. The villagers were perplexed not only by the cow's repeated visits but also by the inexplicable outcome. Upon its return, the cow's udders were found depleted, as if milked, despite the absence of human intervention.

This enigmatic occurrence quickly became the focal point of village discussions, sparking various theories and debates among residents. While some attributed it to divine forces, others sought rational explanations. As the phenomenon persisted, the villagers' curiosity intensified, prompting a deeper investigation.

Driven by a blend of reverence and inquisitiveness, the community decided to unravel the mystery surrounding the cow's actions. They organized a collective effort to excavate the area frequented by the cow. As they dug, anticipation mounted among the gathered onlookers.

Their efforts soon yielded a remarkable discovery. Buried beneath the soil, they unearthed a Shivlinga, a sacred emblem representing Lord Shiva in Hinduism.

This finding was met with awe and veneration, as the villagers interpreted it as a divine sign. The presence of the Shivlinga explained the cow's behavior, aligning with Hindu beliefs regarding the sanctity of cows and their association with deities.

Inspired by this miraculous revelation, the village community felt a sense of divine purpose. They unanimously decided to honor this sacred discovery by constructing a temple dedicated to Lord Shiva at the exact location where the Shivlinga was found.

The construction of the Chaunridhar Temple became a communal endeavor, with villagers contributing their skills, time, and resources. The discovered Shivlinga was carefully extracted and reverently installed as the central deity in the new temple. The temple's architecture and design reflected local artistic traditions while incorporating elements symbolizing its divine origins.

As news of the miraculous discovery and temple construction spread, Chaunridhar began attracting pilgrims and curious visitors from neighboring areas and beyond. The temple evolved into not only a significant place of worship but also a symbol of community unity and faith.

Today, the Chaunridhar Temple stands as a testament to the enduring power of local legends and the deeply rooted spiritual beliefs of the community. It continues to be a revered site, drawing devotees who seek blessings and pay homage to Lord Shiva, while marveling at the extraordinary tale of its inception.

An additional narrative related to the temple concerns the Dhami queen.

The narrative surrounding the temple and the Dhami queen adds a layer of historical and cultural significance to the site. The Princely State of Dhami, situated 26 kilometres west of Shimla, played a role in shaping the temple's legend. As the story of the Shivlinga spread among the local population, it captured the attention of the Dhami queen, who attempted to relocate it to her own temple. The fracturing of the Shivlinga during this attempt was interpreted as a divine intervention, further solidifying the belief in Lord Shiva's presence at the site. This event not only prevented the relocation but also strengthened the local community's connection to the sacred object.

The construction of the temple at this location was a direct response to the perceived supernatural occurrence. It became a focal point for devotees, particularly during the festival of Mahashivratri, when elaborate decorations and rituals are performed. The recitation of mantras, such as:

ॐ युबकं यजामहे सुग पुवध नमः।

उवा वकिमव ब नान्मृ योमु देय मामृतात्॥

which translates to: "Mahadev we offer to you the Tri-Ambakam, the fragrant one, the enhancer of nourishment. Free me from the bondage of death like Urvashi from the nectar." Many devotees have maintained profound reverence for this sacred site. They engaged in the worship of Lord Shiva at this location and sought divine blessings. This continued reverence and worship at the site underscore the enduring nature of faith and the importance of sacred spaces in preserving cultural and religious traditions. The temple's history, intertwined with local legends and royal interventions, has contributed to its status as a significant pilgrimage site, attracting devotees who seek spiritual solace.

Source: The inhabitants of Haridevi narrated this account with considerable zeal.

Quila Mubarak

In the heart of Bathinda city, Punjab, stands one of India's most ancient monuments, a fortress known as 'QUILA MUBARAK'. Constructed by Hindu ruler Raja Dab approximately 2000 years ago, this boat-shaped structure creates an illusion of a ship in the desert. The interior, referred to as 'Androon', once housed members of the Royal Patiala dynasty.

The fort boasted various sections, including Moti palace, Sheesh Mahal, and Jail wala palace, where royal prisoners were confined. One of its kitchen compartments could prepare meals for 35,000 individuals.

Initially, the Mughals called Bathinda city 'TABARHINDH', a Persian term meaning 'the sword of Hindustan'. During the transition of power from Mughal rule, the fort came under Sikh control. Quila Mubarak holds significant importance in Sikh history, as Guru Gobind Singh ji, the tenth Guru, visited to strengthen and unify the Sikh community. His blessing of the fort imbued it with great significance for Sikhs. A tradition called 'Chaalia' persists, where it's believed that wishes come true if one visits the Quila Gurudwara for 40 consecutive days.

The Sutlej River once flowed near Quila Mubarak but changed course over time. A prophecy by Guru Gobind Singh ji suggests the river might return to its original path, potentially causing water-related devastation to the city. This prediction is part of the rich tapestry of Sikh history, showcasing Guru Gobind Singh ji's profound spiritual and temporal insights.

Razia Sultan (1205-1240), the sole female ruler of the Delhi Sultanate in the 13th century, was imprisoned in Quila Mubarak after her dethronement in 1240. Her brief yet notable reign faced opposition from nobles and other factions within the sultanate. Following her betrayal, her half-brother Bahram Shah assumed the throne, facing numerous challenges during his rule.

During her confinement, Razia endured intense emotional turmoil and isolation. Despite multiple escape attempts, she remained captive, ultimately ending her life by leaping from the fort's walls. Local lore suggests that Razia Sultan's spirit still haunts the fort, even though half of it has been transformed into a Gurudwara.

Source: Told by the local people of Bhatinda.

Kali Bari Temple

The Kali Bari Temple in Shimla represents more than a religious sanctuary; it embodies a confluence of mythological, spiritual, and devotional elements. This sacred structure, dedicated to Goddess Kali, serves as a symbol of divine authority and safeguarding. Established in 1845 by Bengali devotees, the temple was originally conceived to honor Shyamala Devi, a manifestation of Kali, from whom Shimla acquired its name. Over time, this religious edifice has become an essential component of the city's cultural and spiritual identity. Furthermore, it is intrinsically connected to the narrative of the Kali Bari Temple's spirit, a tale deeply rooted in religious conviction and the perceived divine intervention of the goddess.

The origins of the Kali Bari Temple can be traced back to a time when the site was engulfed in a lush forest. The area was revered by local inhabitants as the abode of the formidable goddess Shyamala Devi, to whom they offered prayers and small tributes in exchange for her favor and protection. Legends speak of the goddess manifesting herself to her most faithful adherents, offering guidance and shielding them from peril. One such account tells of a devoted follower who experienced a divine vision in his sleep. The goddess instructed him to erect a temple in her name, promising that her spiritual essence would safeguard the region and its people. Deeply moved by this celestial encounter, the devotee shared his experience with others, ultimately leading to the temple's construction. This act of reverence not only brought the Kali Bari Temple into existence but also established the goddess as the spiritual sentinel of the town.

As time passed, the temple's religious importance and the goddess's influence expanded. Many individuals hold the belief that the goddess's spirit actively shields Shimla from disasters. Her essence is thought to dwell within the temple, emitting a strong protective force. Worshippers frequently share stories of experiencing the goddess's divine presence during times of hardship or peril. These experiences, ranging from an unexpected sense of tranquility during personal struggles to unexplained safety in the face of natural calamities, are often attributed to the goddess's blessings.

A captivating myth surrounding the temple recalls a catastrophic tempest that battered Shimla in the early 1900s. The violent storm, with its ferocious winds and torrential downpour, posed an existential threat to the town. As dread swept through the population, an extraordinary event unfolded. At the storm's zenith, a luminous, womanly form manifested above the temple. Astonishingly, the gale force winds diminished and the deluge ceased almost immediately. Eyewitnesses reported that the radiant apparition bore a striking resemblance to the Goddess. This occurrence is now commemorated as a celestial intervention, wherein the essence of the Kali Bari Temple materialized to safeguard the town and its inhabitants from imminent destruction.

A well-known narrative revolves around wanderers who lose their way in the forests surrounding the temple. The tale describes a group of tired pilgrims, unacquainted with the local landscape, who found themselves stranded as night descended. Facing an unclear path forward, they fervently appealed to Goddess Kali for direction. Soon after, a faint illumination appeared in the distance, guiding them safely back to the temple grounds. Upon reaching the sanctuary, the mysterious light vanished, leaving the pilgrims convinced that the goddess's spirit had led them to safety. These accounts have bolstered the conviction that Kali not only dwells within the temple but also extends her protective influence throughout the neighboring areas.

The Kali Bari Temple has become famous for the numerous supernatural events reported by its visitors. Scholars have recorded instances of unexpected recoveries from various medical conditions following prayer sessions at the shrine. Additionally, many worshippers assert that their wishes were granted after making earnest vows to the goddess. These personal narratives have been passed down verbally through successive generations, enhancing the temple's mystical reputation. Visitors often describe experiencing a deep sense of tranquility and vibrant energy when they enter the hallowed grounds, which they believe is due to the omnipresent spirit of the goddess.

The Kali Bari Temple is not only a place of personal significance but also a vital component of Shimla's cultural fabric. During major festivals like Durga Puja and Navratri, the temple becomes a focal point of spiritual activities, attracting devotees from various locations. The atmosphere is charged with the sound of devotional chants and hymns honoring Goddess Kali, creating a palpable sense of devotion. Many locals hold the belief that the Goddess is particularly responsive during these celebratory periods, bestowing her blessings and reinforcing her position as the town's protective deity.

The essence of Kali Bari Temple is intricately woven into Shimla's philosophical outlook. It embodies faith, perseverance, and an unbreakable connection between the goddess and her worshippers. The temple serves as a constant reminder that divine influence can be present in everyday spaces, offering guidance and protection to those who approach with genuine devotion.

The myth surrounding the Kali Bari Temple's spirit continues to flourish, transmitted through spoken narratives and individual encounters. To Shimla's residents, the temple transcended its physical form, embodying their devotion and symbolizing the goddess's lasting influence. The spirit of the Kali Bari Temple remains a crucial element of Shimla's spiritual and cultural identity, manifested through accounts of supernatural assistance, unexpected healings, or the tranquil atmosphere that surrounds the sacred site.

Source: My father shared this story with me.

Bijeshwar Devta Temple

The Bijeshwar Devta Temple is located in Gambharpul, Solan district. Temples dedicated to Bijeshwar Maharaj can also be found in parts of Sirmaur and the former princely states of Bhajji, Baghal, and Keonthal. Interestingly, while some refer to him as Brajeshwar or Brijeshwar, he is referred to as Bijeshwar Mahadev in his Chalisa.

The origin story of the devta's sacred form is documented in his '*ahvahni*' and genealogy, which states:

"O*m Jag Jag Bijeshwar Jai Jai Janma Maas Vaishakhe Sudhi Dashami Dussehra Upje*

Kashi Kashmir Ke Tile Char Chaukdi Ka Raja Bijeshwar Maharaja. Om Jai Dev Biju!"

When a local king's tyranny escalated in Kuthar and nearby regions, residents sought protection from this enlightened being from Kashi, Kashmir. Subsequently, the deity emerged from a reservoir (known as Dabri in the local Pahadi language) on the riverbank. Utilizing his powers to confront the king, a fierce battle ensued.

Eventually, alongside Devta Padyal (his chief minister), Navkothi Durga, and 64 Yoginis, he created a celestial lightning orb. This phenomenon caused earthly tremors, vanquishing ghosts, spirits, and demons. The precise lightning strike compelled the king to retreat from battle. Consequently, he became known as Bijeshwar Mahadev, clarifying the meaning of "Bijo Ra Gola" in this context.

Following these events, the devta's abode was established in Devthal itself, as per his blessings and directives.

The devta's appearance includes earrings, a pearl necklace in his hair, and a snake draped around his neck, reminiscent of Mahadev. His mode of transport is a white horse, and he bears an umbrella above his head. These details are derived from the genealogical records.

Notably, those who consider Bijeshwar Maharaj their Isht Dev must perform Karyala during the birth or marriage of their eldest son. Bijeshwar Maharaj presides over Karyaale ceremonies. He once subdued Mata Chandravali, who was intoxicated with pride and power, cursing her to dance in every courtyard. This explains why Karyaale ceremonies begin with Chandravali's dance.

This picturesque site is situated approximately 8 km from Kunihar, on the Dharmpur or Solan road, and 1 km from Gambharpul on the Shimla Road, where his original place stands. The temple, constructed on the riverbank, is enhanced by the river's beauty. Its architecture resembles a royal palace, complete with a beautiful saraha within the temple complex.

Source: This narrative was recounted by my grandfather.

The Tale of Dhola and Maru

I n the arid region of Rajasthan, characterized by its golden sands and where atmospheric conditions facilitated the transmission of historical romantic narratives, there resided a princess named Maru. She was the offspring of King Pingal, a monarch of a territory renowned for its courageous warriors and inhospitable desert landscape. Her physical attributes were widely acknowledged: eyes reminiscent of desert oases in their depth, hair comparable to the nocturnal sky in its darkness, and a disposition as unblemished as the revered waters of Pushkar. During Maru's early developmental years, she was formally promised in marriage to Prince Dhola of Narwar, a kingdom recognized for its noble rulers and impressive architectural structures.

The betrothal was celebrated with great anticipation, as many believed their bond would herald an age of tranquility and wealth for both kingdoms. However, the intricate tapestry of fate had other designs in store. As the years unfolded and Dhola matured, the commitments of his youth faded from his consciousness. The ruler of Narwar, Dhola's father, arranged his marriage to another royal daughter, causing the memory of his promised bride to dissipate like mist in the morning sun. Concurrently, in Pugal, Maru evolved into a captivating young woman, eagerly awaiting the moment when Dhola would arrive to fulfill their childhood pledge. Alas, that moment never materialized.

Devastated but determined, Maru enlisted the aid of a traveling minstrel who often performed in Narwar's royal courts. She crafted a poignant ballad, infusing her anguish into harmonies that expressed her eternal devotion and a pledge once sworn. Moved by her commitment, the minstrel vowed to deliver her composition to Dhola, reminding him of his forgotten oath. Upon reaching Dhola's palace, the minstrel performed Maru's emotional tale, awakening something profound within the prince's soul. Recollections suppressed by obligation and the passage of time emerged—of a princess from the desert whose gaze conveyed endless yearning. Dhola's heart filled with remorse and desire, compelling him to rectify his mistake. Despite his current spouse's objections and backed by his faithful followers, Dhola embarked on a journey to Pugal, eager to reunite with Maru.

Their fated love, however, was not without its trials. During Dhola's expedition across the treacherous Thar Desert, rival leaders schemed to prevent a union that would strengthen both realms. Among them was Uma, the Jaisalmer sovereign, who feared Maru's charm and influence might eclipse his own. He deployed spies and mercenaries to intercept Dhola's entourage, aiming to derail the journey before it truly began.

Meanwhile, Maru confronted her own challenges. King Pingal, her father, had grown doubtful of Dhola's prolonged absence and was hesitant to entrust his daughter to someone who seemed to have forgotten her for years. Nonetheless, Maru's resolve remained unshaken. She beseeched her father, declaring, "A vow of love should not be discarded. Permit me to follow my destiny, for my heart recognizes its true path."

Dhola eventually reached Pugal, fatigued yet unwavering in his determination. The moment he laid eyes on Maru, all his uncertainties, apprehensions, and the lengthy separation vanished. He pledged to remain by her side eternally.

Their bliss was short-lived, as Uma's followers ambushed their caravan en route to Narwar. Encircled by Uma's forces in the desert's expanse, Maru exhibited her ingenuity and valor, leveraging her desert wisdom to outmaneuver their assailants. She dispatched a message to neighboring Rajput clans loyal to her lineage, igniting a fierce battle. The desert winds carried the clamor of clashing swords, and ultimately, Dhola and Maru's love emerged victorious.

The couple's triumphant return to Narwar marked the beginning of their reign, characterized by keen judgment and genuine concern for their subjects. Their remarkable journey became a cherished folk tale, handed down through generations and performed by wandering bards across Rajasthan, exemplifying the unyielding strength and commitment of true love. To this day, the "Dhola Maru" legend continues to captivate listeners during desert evenings, embodying love's timeless power to overcome temporal, geographical, and even predestined obstacles.

Source:https://digital.amarchitrakatha.com/id005835189/D hola-And-Maru

Story narrated by a person from Rajasthan.

Dhola Maru

> The Dhola Maru tale honours Maru's loyalty and patience, Dhola's naliance, and their undying love for each other.".

The tale of Dhola, a prince from Narwar, and Princess Maru of Poogal, belongs to the Kachhwaha tradition. King Pingal, who governed the small realm of Poogal, decided to send his young daughter Maru to wed Dhola, the son of King Nal of Narwar, his ally. Although child marriages are now illegal, Maru and Dhola were betrothed as children. Following Nal's death, Dhola abandoned his commitment to Maru, who was still an infant, and married Malwani instead. Despite King Pingal's numerous attempts to contact Dhola, Maru couldn't reunite with him as Malwani thwarted all communication efforts. Eventually, Maru reached Dhola through a group of folk performers, prompting him to rush to Poogal upon learning of his first wife's existence. However, the cunning Malwani was determined to prevent their reunion.

As Dhola prepared to marry, Malwani fabricated a message claiming Maru had died, urging him to return immediately. Dhola, not entirely under Malwani's influence, recognized the deception and continued with his plans. During his journey to Poogal, he encountered Umar Sumar, a bandit leader who falsely claimed Maru had been sold into another marriage. Umar Sumar harbored a strong interest in Maru. Upon arriving in Poogal, Dhola was greeted by the citizens, and ur satyavadi married dhola maru amidst mounting tension.

On their return to Narwar, Maru was bitten by a snake in the desert and perished. Overwhelmed with grief and anger, Dhola considered becoming the first male to perform sati, a custom typically reserved for Rajput women. However, a yogi and yogini intervened just in time to prevent this act.

Despite Umar Samar's earlier promise to reform, he once again invited the unsuspecting couple while still infatuated with Maru. This time, folk singers warned them of the dacoits' malicious intentions. Consequently, the couple escaped on a camel, hastening to Malwa, where they ultimately lived happily with Malwani.

Source: https://en.wikipedia.org/wiki/Dhola_Maru

Elders of Rajasthan.

The Story of Baz Bahadur and Roopmati

This is the tale of the love between Roopmati, a singing shepherdess who would later become the queen of Malwa, and the Sultan Baz Bahadur. This story recounts a royal union devoid of political motives or passion, yet it symbolizes a connection between Islamic and Hindu cultures.

Baz Bahadur, the last independent ruler of Mandu, was deeply passionate about music. During a hunting expedition, he was captivated by a woman's singing. Following the enchanting voice, he instantly fell for both her melodious tones and striking appearance. Upon witnessing Roopmati and her companions singing and reveling, Baz Bahadur became enamored with her.

Enchanted by her melodious voice and stunning beauty, he asked for her hand in marriage and invited her to his capital, Mandau. She agreed to accompany him on the condition that he construct a palace allowing her to view her cherished Narmada River. This led to the creation of the Rewa Kund reservoir and Roopmati Pavilion. Baz Bahadur built the kund to ensure Rani Roopmati's constant access to water, with an aqueduct supplying water throughout the structure. The awe-inspiring

Rupmati's Pavilion offered her views of Baz Bahadur's Palace and the Narmada River.

Roopmati eventually reciprocated his feelings, likely due to their shared passion for poetry and music. As a singer herself, she was drawn to his lyrical and musical talents. Their marriage, celebrated in both Hindu and Muslim traditions, was commemorated with the construction of her palace. Their bond grew so strong that Baz Bahadur found himself more devoted to love and music than to his royal duties.

The Mughal emperor Akbar, also known as Akbar the Great, took notice of Baz Bahadur's neglect of his kingdom, having heard rumors of Rani Roopmati's beauty. He sent his general's brother, Adham Khan, to lead a massive invasion.

In 1561, Baz Bahadur and Adham Khan clashed in Sarangpur. Realizing his small army stood no chance, Baz Bahadur chose to flee Mandu rather than face defeat and death. In his haste, he inadvertently left Roopmati behind.

Upon learning of these events, the loyal Roopmati understood that Adham Khan would soon come for her. She decided to poison herself before he could dishonor her. Baz Bahadur survived for a few more years after this tragedy.

His fate remains uncertain, with two possible endings: either he perished in a subsequent attack or surrendered to Akbar and joined his army.

In the end, Roopmati exercised a rare choice for women of her time by deciding her own fate. The courageous Roopmati's memory lived on in people's hearts, while the Sultan of Malwa remained a fugitive for years to come.

Source: A friend from Rajasthan.

The Unknown Encounter

In the tranquil village of Chak Chtana, situated in Ludhiana district's core, there lived a modest and devout individual called Jaswinder Singh. Each day at dawn, during the revered Amrit Vela, Jaswinder would embark on a journey to the nearby Gurudwara Shri Katana Sahib, riding his aging bicycle. The era lacked proper roadways, leaving only meandering trails through expansive croplands. Jaswinder's trek was extensive, often leading him through dimly lit areas illuminated solely by his carried lantern. This particular morning, like all others, Jaswinder pedaled while concentrating on sacred hymns, his spirit serene with reverence. A low-lying fog enveloped the landscape, and the atmosphere was rich with the soil's aroma. As he traversed the fields, he detected something out of the ordinary—a silhouette looming in the distance, partially obscured by the haze. The entity wore lengthy, worn shawls and archaic attire that seemed to belong to a bygone century, as if it had materialized from a long-forgotten time.

Jaswinder's bicycle gradually came to a halt as he elevated the lantern to improve his visibility. The enigmatic figure's countenance remained cloaked in darkness, yet there was an uncanny and vaguely recognizable aspect to the scene. Though not overtly threatening, the surrounding quietude caused Jaswinder's heartbeat to accelerate. Nonetheless, as a devout individual, he pushed aside his discomfort. He speculated that the person might have acquired these weathered garments from some unknown source. Despite his extensive life experiences, this encounter stood out as unique. Upon approaching, the figure addressed him in a deep, husky voice, "I'm also en route to the Gurudwara. Might I trouble you for a ride?" Jaswinder acquiesced with a polite nod, signaling the figure to join him on the bicycle. Without uttering a word, the stranger mounted the cycle, and they embarked on their journey together. Over the course of 30 to 40 minutes, as they traversed fields with the faint sound of a distant river, the stranger disclosed, "I've traversed these lands for years, in pursuit of inner peace and enlightenment," he began, his tone unnaturally composed, "I too once sought spiritual awakening, but I lost my way. My conscience is burdened with regrets, and now I wander in search of serenity."

As a compassionate individual, Jaswinder listened intently to the stranger's account of life's tribulations, lost affection, and profound melancholy. A wave of empathy washed over him for the man. Continuing his journey, Jaswinder's attention oscillated between his responsibilities and the ongoing dialogue, detecting no malevolence in the shared narrative. However, as they neared Gurudwara Sahib, an inexplicable sensation began to permeate the atmosphere. The surrounding air grew increasingly oppressive, and an eerie silence seemed to descend upon them. While Jaswinder still perceived the familiar weight of his passenger on the bicycle, he noticed a peculiar change as they approached the Gurudwara's entrance. The bicycle, once burdened by an additional rider, suddenly felt remarkably light.

Glancing over his shoulder, Jaswinder was astounded to find that the stranger who had been accompanying him moments ago had inexplicably vanished. A shiver of disbelief coursed through his body. His lantern flickered frantically as he abruptly halted the bicycle, scanning the vicinity with bewildered eyes. The mysterious figure had disappeared without a trace. The mist thickened, leaving only the gentle whisper of wind through the crops. Jaswinder's heart raced as he grappled with the incomprehensible event. Had his mind conjured an illusion? Could the tranquil morning hours be playing tricks on his senses?

Jaswinder gazed at the bicycle, feeling the cool metal under his fingertips, then turned his attention back to the Gurudwara. Everything appeared normal, yet the man had vanished without a trace, leaving no footprints or evidence of his presence. A profound sense of disquiet settled over Jaswinder as he stood there. While his spiritual path had always been one of tranquility and devotion, this encounter felt different, as if something otherworldly had touched him, leaving behind an air of enigma. He offered a silent prayer and bowed reverently.

Upon entering the Gurudwara Sahib, tranquility returned, but his mind remained troubled. The mysterious figure, his cryptic words, and sudden disappearance seemed to hint at a deeper meaning, perhaps a divine lesson.

In the years that followed, Jaswinder often shared this experience with his fellow villagers, though he never fully grasped its significance. Some believed it was a spirit seeking guidance, while others thought it might be an ancient soul in search of redemption. Each day, as he passed the field where the encounter occurred, Jaswinder would light a small diya at the exact location, offering prayers for the stranger's peace, despite never seeing him again.

Many years later, Jaswinder discussed the incident with the head of Gurudwara Sahib. After a moment of contemplation, the head priest revealed a startling fact: "Jaswinder Singh, there's a grave near that spot belonging to a man who died in the early 1800s. He was a wanderer, much like the man you encountered. Legend has it that he died seeking atonement for his life's misdeeds. Since his death, many villagers have reported sightings of his spirit, lost and searching for peace, roaming those fields."

A shiver ran down Jaswinder's spine as he realized the man he had met was no ordinary traveler, but the spirit of a lost soul, still wandering the earth in search of the peace that eluded him in life. The following morning, as Jaswinder passed the same field, he noticed something unusual: a solitary white lily blooming where he had once encountered the stranger. As he knelt down, an overwhelming sense of peace washed over him, as if the spirit had finally found solace. In the quiet morning air,

Jaswinder heard a faint whisper, almost indistinguishable from the wind, gently saying, "Thank you." The atmosphere seemed to lighten in that moment.

The uncanny encounter, initially frightening, concluded in an unforeseen and serene manner, with the spirit finally achieving its long-awaited absolution. The incident remained etched in the collective memory of Chak Chtana's inhabitants, and accounts of the peculiar individual who accompanied Jaswinder Singh circulated throughout the village. To this day, every youngster in the community is familiar with the narrative, which the elders recount with a blend of amazement and deference. The once-eerie field has been transformed into consecrated ground. As a gesture of respect for the wandering spirit, the villagers adorned the area with a revered Nishan Sahib, rendering it inaccessible to visitors. It has since become a site of hushed veneration, where the corporeal and ethereal realms seemingly intersect, their boundary marked by the sacred fabric of the Nishan Sahib gently undulating in the breeze.

The peculiar incident involving Jaswinder Singh has transformed into a treasured family anecdote, transmitted across generations. I initially learned of this account while spending a summer at my maternal grandmother's home. On a serene evening, as we observed the adjacent fields from the porch, my uncle recounted the story to me in his rich, deep voice.

Source: This tale was narrated to me by a family member.

www.ingramcontent.com/pod-product-compliance
Lightning Source LLC
LaVergne TN
LVHW041846070526
838199LV00045BA/1463